MORE THAN DEVOTION

Fifty-Days of Remembrance and Resolve

JUDY SALISBURY

LOGOS PRESENTATIONS
EQUIPPING - MOTIVATING - LIFE CHANGING

Published by
Logos Presentations
Woodland, WA

More than Devotion: Fifty-Days of Remembrance and Resolve
by Judy Salisbury

Published by Logos Presentations
Woodland, WA 98674

ISBN: 9798642339107

Endorsements

More than Devotion is full of awesome encouragement from God's Word coupled with practical experiences and applications from years of walking in the "cool of the day" with God. It is not just another devotional; Judy captures the very essence of how Scripture applies to our everyday life—past, present, and future. I loved it!

PASTOR DENNY MARTINEZ Former Senior Pastor, Calvary Chapel Woodland, Woodland, WA

As a busy clergyman in the Lord's Service, I can connect with these devotions. It is so easy to suffer burnout from ministry. The constant need to give out from being needed to feed and nurture others around me can be draining at times. The time of quiet rest with the Father and His Word is food and drink for my soul. Judy Salisbury, in this book, provides an oasis for ministry leaders or lay Christian alike. She interweaves stories, Scripture, theology, and applicable lessons that we can use in our lives. I encourage the reader to take time as they read and drink from the fountain of God's Word here in her 50-days of refreshing. Take time to meditate upon what she is saying and write out the "My Task/Challenge" and "My Outcome/Results" at the end of each day's connection with God. I believe that you will grow in a closer relationship and understanding of God and His Word.

THOMAS F. MARSHALL, D.MIN, THD, DBC, BCPC, Minister, Author, Christian Educator, Chaplain, Board Certified Pastoral Counselor

*The strength of **More than Devotion** lies in its solid biblical foundation, which Judy Salisbury has diligently studied, accurately conveyed, and conveniently applied to our daily life experiences. Judy brilliantly and beautifully parallels Old and New Testament passages for each life lesson, reminding us of God's power, God's plan, and God's promises. For fifty days, familiar Scriptures and*

Judy's valuable insight stirred my soul and strengthened my faith. I trust it will do the same for you.

JENNIFER SANDS, 9/11 Widow
Christian author and speaker

Judy Salisbury's book is fittingly entitled **More than Devotion**. This unique work prompts the reader to take practical actions that can grow us up into better followers of Christ and people in general. Her daily use of similar accounts from the Old and New Testaments not only helps us to become more familiar with biblical personalities, their struggles, and their successes with remarkable relevance for us all, but her approach also develops in the reader a greater love and appreciation for the Word of God. I happily give my hearty endorsement to this work and pray everyone who is serious about growing in the Lord reads it!

ANGELA COURTE MACKENZIE
host, SuperChannel TV; Founder, Amazing Women

Although **More than Devotion** features the time between our Lord's Resurrection and Pentecost, Salisbury's compelling devotions are also an invaluable resource for centering your thoughts on Christ during the fifty days before Easter. Daily Old and New Testament readings combine with thoughtful reflections and timeless truths that deepen faith and inspire a walk of intimacy on your journey to the Lenten Cross.

GAIL WELBORN
Book & Audio Review Columnist, *Seattle Examiner*

Dedicated to my beloved son,

Mikael:

My son, observe the commandment of your father
And do not forsake the teaching of your mother;
Bind them continually on your heart;
Tie them around your neck.
When you walk about, they will guide you;
When you sleep, they will watch over you;
And when you awake, they will talk to you.
For the commandment is a lamp and the teaching is light;
And reproofs for discipline are the way of life.
—PROVERBS 6:20–23

I could not be prouder of the man you have become
since the original publication of this work in 2015.
I am amazed and thankful for the many lives you've impacted
and poured into thus far. I know as you remain in the Lord's palm,
nothing shall be impossible to you. Truly, you can do ALL things
through Christ, Who gives you strength. I love you so much!
You are a total joy to me.
With tremendous love and affection,

Mom

Contents

Acknowledgments

My heart is filled with gratitude to my spiritual mom, Lola Crawford. Before going home to be with Jesus in 2019, she endured first-draft reviews of this work. Her counsel proved amazingly appropriate for not only this work but for my life as well!

I much appreciate Joan Phillip's original editing of this work. I learn something new each time she conducts her magic. Trust me, with my rough drafts; she needs a big wand! Thanks also to Rachel Starr Thomson for her excellent and timely editorial work on this project as well.

Many thanks to Pastor Denny Martinez for the impact he made on my ministry and life as a mentor for twenty-five years. I so appreciate his endorsement of this work before going home to be with the Lord in 2017.

Special thanks to those who also endorsed this work—Thomas F. Marshall, Angela Courte Mackenzie, Jennifer Sands, and Gail Welborn—for your kind, encouraging words.

Deepest thanks to my beloved husband, Jeff. He is a wonderful man who, for over three decades, has been thoroughly entertained by the fact that I can't sit still except when I'm writing. Jeff, no words can adequately express my love and appreciation for you, or describe your impact in helping me believe that "I can do all things through Him who strengthens me."[1]

All praise and honor to my Almighty Heavenly Father, Who brought beauty from ashes by helping me produce a work I can place at Jesus's feet. I pray it will ignite a burning passion for You, and Your Word, and a life-changing awareness toward obedience for those who genuinely desire to be "fit vessels" for Your kingdom and glory!

---

[1] Philippians 4:13

Before You Begin

Come and let us recount in Zion
The work of the LORD our God!
—JEREMIAH 51:10

⸺⸺⸺⸺⸺⸺⸺⸺⸺⸺⸺⸺⸺⸺⸺⸺⸺⸺⸺⸺⸺⸺⸺⸺

*A*s you embark on this devotional book, there are a few features of this effort I wish to draw to your attention before you begin. It is important to point out that I did not title this book with the words *more than* as a hook to attain more readers, but because it does contain and accomplish more than what you might be accustomed to when reaching for a devotional book. In light of this, I feel it is important to outline its uniqueness.

What might catch your attention immediately is that it is not a 31-day or 365-day devotional, but rather, 50-days. The reason for this is because that time frame appears to be important to God. Therefore, it ought to be important for us as well.

Consider the fifty days between the resurrection of Jesus, Yeshua the Messiah, until the day of Pentecost. As we read in Acts 2, it was during Penticost that both Jew and Gentile became one dynamic body of believers. I imagine a lot of personal growth, revelation, and spiritual maturity occurred within the apostles during those fifty days from Passover, the time of our Lord's crucifixion, to Pentecost.

Consider the two disciples, or *talmidim*, and our Lord on the road to Emmaus. What occurred during that journey is the subjects of my book, *The Emmaus Conversation*, and was the motivation to write this companion devotional.

The two men began their journey deeply downcast and confused after seeing their Lord first hailed as king and then tortured, crucified, and buried in the same week. To hear from women—not an acceptable means of reliable communication in that culture and time—that His body was missing from the tomb must have especially distressed them. Yet, when Yeshua in veiled form unexpectedly walked with those two disciples on their sorrowful journey, He taught them, preparing future leaders for service. As He, "beginning with Moses and with all the prophets, explained to them the things concerning Himself in all the Scriptures."[2]

In an instant, at the breaking of bread with their Messiah, not only were the physical eyes of the two disciples opened but also their spiritual eyes. No wonder they dashed back to Jerusalem to proclaim with joy the reality of Jesus' resurrection and that He was, indeed, the Messiah! Scripture tells us:

> To these He also presented Himself alive after His suffering, by many convincing proofs, appearing to them over a period of forty days and speaking of the things concerning the kingdom of God. Gathering them together, He commanded them not to leave Jerusalem, but to wait for what the Father had promised. "Which," He said, "you heard of from Me."[3]

During those forty days after the Lamb of God was slain and rose again, the apostles learned directly from Him. They observed face-to-face the evidence of His resurrection from the dead, and they finally understood that all the prophets foretold concerning the Messiah was realized in Yeshua, Jesus.

I imagine during the ten days after Jesus' ascension, the apostles recounted the evidence and remembered what they witnessed concerning Him. Perhaps they prepared for fellowship on a mass scale, readying their hearts and minds for the discipleship of new converts.

These ever-important fifty days before Pentecost (*Shavuot* for our Jewish friends) became a time of personal growth and preparation for the apostles. Since they grew spiritually during the days from Passover to Pentecost, we can also make it a meaningful time of personal growth and preparation for His work and will as well.

Throughout this devotional, each day begins with Scripture imploring us to *remember* something. It amazes me how often our Lord God reminds us not to forget. He knows that remembering even important things can be a challenge for us. After all, how

---

[2] Luke 24:27
[3] Acts 1:3–4

often do we walk into a room and forget the reason why once there? We forget important dates unless we upload them into our smartphones to help us remember with annoying notifications. And amidst the busyness, we seem to forget what and *Who* is most important along the way.

God knows our frailty in this area, and so He calls us to remember a host of things, including His great and mighty deeds throughout history. He also wants us to remember various individuals in the Scriptures—their specific circumstances and how He dealt with them.

Remembering is important for many reasons. Before we can proclaim or recount to others what God has accomplished in our lives, before we can share His works and majesty, we must first remember them. As you read this devotional, you will find many individuals recounting important facets of history to their audiences. I can also list a host of reasons for remembering and recounting the goodness and power of God. However, you should move through these fifty days learning for yourself how important it is to remember. As you will see, to remember is evidently a divine command.

There is another feature of this resource that you will find helpful. After reading an opening Scripture passage that calls you to *remember* or *consider* something, you will then read a related account from the Old Testament or Old Covenant, then a similar or related account from the New Testament or New Covenant.

Just as Jew and Gentile formed into one new body on Pentecost, I have melded accounts from the Old and New Covenants into one day of solid encouragement, teaching, and devotion. Within this framework, you will notice people are the same. Since we struggle in the same areas, no doubt, you will relate to one or all of the biblical personalities and their circumstances on many levels. Through this approach, you will also see God is the same in all places and at all times. He is the same God in the Old Covenant as He is in the New. The same Messiah of Whom the prophets foretold in the Old Covenant walked among believers in the New. His desire is the same for us: our repentance for the forgiveness of our sins, a new life in Him on earth, and utter joy with Him for all eternity.

I pray you will find this devotional stimulating, eye-opening, convicting, and perhaps even life-changing. It most certainly will be if you follow through with the *"My Task/Challenge"* and *"My Outcome/Results,"* at the end of each day's reading. I pray you will explore remembrance not only during the days between Passover and Shavuot but also at other times throughout the year.

May the Lord Jesus, Yeshua our Messiah, bless you, as you allow Him to use this resource for personal and spiritual growth, remembering and recounting to many others the lessons He has taught you.

Your sister and servant in Yeshua, Jesus our Messiah,
Judy Salisbury

DAY 1 ~ *God Keeps His Promises*

*"When the bow is in the cloud, then I will look upon it,
to remember the everlasting covenant between God and
every living creature of all flesh that is on the earth."*
—GENESIS 9:16

You are driving in your vehicle when suddenly it appears! Your passengers lean across each other to catch a glimpse. You would do the same, but somebody needs to keep their eyes on the road. It is simply awe-inspiring, no matter how many times it appears. In all its brilliance adorning the sky, the rainbow calls us to *remember*.

When my children were small, I taught them the meaning of the rainbow. Every time one appeared, I would point it out, saying, "What does the rainbow mean?" My children would then excitedly, and confidently reply, "God keeps His promises." Indeed, He does. Does God need a reminder? No, He surely does not. However, those He created in His image do need reminders that He is a covenant-keeping God.

It is certainly an incredible concept to grasp. An ultra-dimensional, omnipotent, omniscient, omnipresent Being condescended to covenant with His creatures. Yet, He did. Not only did He establish an *everlasting covenant* with Noah and all his descendants (the entire human race), but also *every living creature* with him and his family on the big barge we call the ark. God promised Noah:

> "I establish My covenant with you; and all flesh shall never again be cut off by the water of the flood, neither shall there again be a flood to destroy the earth."[4]

After this promise, God did not stop covenanting with people whom He created in His image. Generations passed, and humanity scattered at the Tower of Babel. Many wandered from God. Still,

---

[4] Genesis 9:11

5

He remained faithful to His people and made another covenant. God promised a man named Abram:

> "I will establish My covenant between Me and you and your descendants after you throughout their generations for an everlasting covenant, to be God to you and to your descendants after you. I will give to you and to your descendants after you, the land of your sojournings, all the land of Canaan, for an everlasting possession; and I will be their God."[5]

Something evident jumps off the page after reading the account associated with the Abrahamic covenant. This covenant was to pass down to Abram's *descendants*. This promise challenged Abram, later known as Abraham, because, after many years of marriage, he remained childless.

Abram's wife Sarai, later known as Sarah, was well beyond childbearing years. Yet God kept His promise. After some turbulent times for Abram, running ahead of God to fulfill this promise (Oh, the mistakes we make when we refuse to rest in God's timing!), Sarai gave birth to little Isaac, the child of the promise.

Many generations later, God covenanted with another servant, King David. The Lord then promised through the prophet, Nathan, that another child would be born. However, this child would be the coming king.

> "When your days are complete and you lie down with your fathers, I will raise up your descendant after you, who will come forth from you, and I will establish his kingdom. He shall build a house for My name, and I will establish the throne of his kingdom forever."[6]

Again, time passed until Jeremiah prophesied:

> "Behold, days are coming," declares the LORD, "when I will make a new covenant with the house of Israel and with the house of Judah . . . I will put My law within them and on their heart I will write it; and I will be their God, and they shall be My people. They will not teach

---

[5] Genesis 17:7-8
[6] 2 Samuel 7:12–13

again, each man his neighbor and each man his brother, saying, 'know the LORD,' for they will all know Me, from the least of them to the greatest of them," declares the LORD, "for I will forgive their iniquity, and their sin I will remember no more."[7]

Our covenant-keeping God does not change His mind. He does not go back on what He promises. He reiterates His promises throughout Scripture. He fulfills His covenants. God keeps His promises.

Centuries later, in an upper room, Jesus lifted a cup, the cup of redemption. He explained:

> "This cup which is poured out for you is the new covenant in My blood[8] . . . Drink from it, all of you; for this is My blood of the covenant, which is poured out for many for forgiveness of sins."[9]

Jesus, Yeshua the Messiah, established a New Covenant so that whoever believes in Him will receive eternal life. Isn't it astonishing that God—who cannot lie, who never changes—lovingly draws all who believe, including you, into His everlasting New Covenant?

God keeps His promises. Do you? Is there something you promised someone, or perhaps to yourself, that you neglect to keep? Did you promise God something that is still unfulfilled? The Old Covenant cautions, "If a man makes a vow to the LORD, or takes an oath to bind himself with a binding obligation, he shall not violate his word; he shall do according to all that proceeds out of his mouth."[10]

However, as frail human beings, we can become caught up in the passion of the moment. Because we are not as faithful as God in keeping promises or paying vows, we find this advice in His Word: "When you make a vow to God, do not be late in paying it; for He takes no delight in fools. Pay what you vow! It is better

---

[7] Jeremiah 31:31, 33–34
[8] Luke 22:20
[9] Matthew 26:27–28
[10] Numbers 30:2

that you should not vow than that you should vow and not pay."[11]

If it is within your ability to keep a vow, take a step toward fulfilling it today. If it resides outside your power to do so, be honest with yourself and those to whom you made a vow or covenant. Humbly admit your frailty and ask for forgiveness. We all fail, but we can remember that God provided for our forgiveness, not just in this area but in all areas. If neglecting to fulfill a vow is an obstacle for you, simply confess it to the Lord. Then take Solomon's wise advice: It is better not to make a vow at all!

*Not one of the good promises which the LORD
had made to the house of Israel failed; All came to pass.*
—JOSHUA 21:45

---

[11] Ecclesiastes 5:4-5

My Task/Challenge

_____
_____
_____
_____
_____
_____
_____
_____
_____
_____

My Outcome/Results

_____
_____
_____
_____
_____
_____
_____
_____
_____
_____
_____
_____

DAY 2 ~ *No Turning Back*

"Remember this day in which you went out from Egypt, from the house of slavery; for by a powerful hand the LORD brought you out from this place."
—EXODUS 13:3

*M*oses uttered a powerful reminder to the Israelites as they faced the Red Sea. God wanted His people to remember their deliverance from Egypt.

It is hard to imagine how they could forget four-hundred years of misery that their people endured in Egypt. How could they ever forget the dreadful plagues upon the Egyptians, one after another, that finally prompted Pharaoh's hardened heart to let Israel escape into the wilderness to worship their God? In actuality, the Lord's mighty hand let Israel go, not Pharaoh's scepter.

The enemy wielded no power over the children of Israel except for what the Lord allowed. The plagues served as a judgment upon a hardened heart. Yet amid chaos, God instituted a ceremony that final, dreadful night in Egypt: the first of many Passover celebrations. After deliverance, Passover perpetually reminds His people about their freedom from Egypt, recounting the Lord's mighty hand to future generations.

For those of us with new lives in Jesus, we can remember the slavery of our personal Egypt. We ought always to remember how, by the Lord's great and loving hand, He drew us into His glorious freedom.

For me, the time of deliverance was December 1991 in Morgan Hill, California. I had worked there as I traveled while in sales and *happened* to stumble upon a Christian radio talk show as I drove from appointment to appointment. God drew me to Himself through Dr. Walter Martin, as I listen to a debate between himself and a cultist regarding the deity of Jesus. That debate took place years before I heard it as a rebroadcast; however, it was the first time evidence on this topic had confronted me. I had always assumed Yeshua's deity was something for which there was no evidence.

Convicted, I quickly returned to my hotel room, wondering where to turn in the Bible placed in the bedside table drawer by a faithful Gideon International member.[12] The Holy Spirit in His wisdom led me to First John, and at that moment, God plucked me from living as a slave to sin and impulse into a life filled with joy and freedom in Him. Yeshua said:

> "Truly, truly, I say to you, everyone who commits sin is the slave of sin. The slave does not remain in the house forever; the son does remain forever. So if the Son makes you free, you will be free indeed."[13]

Free indeed—an accurate description.

Moses implored the newly freed children of Israel to remember their release from slavery by God. Unfortunately, it did not take long for them to forget. So often, when we read accounts of the Israelites' rebellion, turning to idolatry and blatant unbelief, we shake our head and think, *How could they rebel like that after all God did for them?* Yet we can behave just like the children of Israel. The apostle Paul, through the inspiration of the Holy Spirit, understood our capacity for rebellion. He admonished:

> But now that you have come to know God, or rather to be known by God, how is it that you turn back again to the weak and worthless elemental things, to which you desire to be enslaved all over again?[14]

How easily we can forget when life caves in around us. How easily we forget when circumstances in our lives do not "click" as we envisioned. In contrast, when life turns in our favor, success can blind us, and we deceive ourselves into believing it will never end. We feel tempted to turn back again to things that enslaved us as before.

---

[12] For information on their wonderful work, please visit: http://www.gideons.org/
[13] John 8:34–36
[14] Galatians 4:9

Because we can so quickly regress in our walk with the Lord, the Apostle Paul also reminded us:

> Do you not know that when you present yourselves to someone as slaves for obedience, you are slaves of the one whom you obey, either of sin resulting in death, or of obedience resulting in righteousness? But thanks be to God that though you were slaves of sin, you became obedient from the heart to that form of teaching to which you were committed, and having been freed from sin, you became slaves of righteousness.[15]

What an exchange—from a slave of sin to a slave of righteousness! How we live, and the attitudes we express, reveal which master we have chosen.

Have you forgotten how the Lord drew you out of your Egypt by His powerful and delivering hand? Are you drawn back again toward what once enslaved you instead of living free for His glorious purposes? Ask yourself, *Is there anything in my life I've allowed to enslave me again?* If so, let it go. Enjoy your freedom in Jesus. Be still and allow Him to show you what it could be, allow Him to convict your heart and then move accordingly by His power.

"No longer do I call you slaves . . .
but I have called you friends."
—JOHN 15:15

---

[15] Romans 6:16–18

My Task/Challenge

My Outcome/Results

DAY 3 ~ *The Substance of the Sabbath*

"Remember the sabbath day, to keep it holy."
—EXODUS 20:8

*D*uring the early days of their wilderness journey, just over two months after leaving Egypt, direct from heaven, God provided something special for the children of Israel to eat. Upon seeing the wafers, which had the appearance of dew on the ground in the early morning hours, the Israelites proclaimed, "*Man hu?*" or "What is it?"[16] For five days, they were to gather their manna. However, on the sixth day, they were to gather twice as much. The provision of manna would not appear on the seventh day because God had declared the Sabbath a day unto Himself, a day of complete rest.

At first, some Israelites did not listen and neglected to collect two days' worth on day six. To their amazement, God meant what He said. They found no manna on day seven. Perhaps the Israelites thought if they did not work on the Sabbath, they would starve. Perhaps they did not believe God would provide food for them. However, He knew the importance of setting aside that day of complete rest.

The fourth of the Ten Commandments addressed this directive about the Sabbath:

"Remember the sabbath day, to keep it holy. Six days you shall labor and do all your work, but the seventh day is a sabbath of the LORD your God; in it you shall not do any work, you or your son or your daughter, your male or your female servant or your cattle or your sojourner who stays with you.

"For in six days the LORD made the heavens and the earth, the sea and all that is in them, and rested on the

---

[16] Exodus 16:12-31

14

seventh day; therefore the LORD blessed the sabbath day and made it holy."[17]

You might be wondering, *Did God really need a day for personal rest?* The answer, of course, is no. Nevertheless, He knew *we* did. God created the Sabbath as a day of complete rest. What a foreign concept for our hustle-and-bustle world. The Lord knows we need time to be quiet, to be attentive when He speaks to our hearts. Rest offers a chance for renewal, recovery, and reflection.

How unfortunate that many people either ignore this day or are legalistic in their observance. God told us to *celebrate* the Sabbath. We are not to worship the day, but the Creator of the day. How sad that for some folks it is reduced to a day for duty, like paying taxes, when in reality we *get* to—we take the opportunity to—celebrate the Sabbath.

As usual, humanity seems to taint just about everything. If we can take an opposing stance, we do our best to argue, no matter the outcome. We grow divisive over days as Jesus recognized in the legalists of His day when certain religionists perverted the Sabbath. His response focused on those who missed the purpose of the day and the One who created it. Jesus rebuked, "The Sabbath was made for man, and not man for the Sabbath. So the Son of Man is Lord even of the Sabbath."[18]

After this reminder, the Lord put the Pharisees' legalism to the test:

> [Jesus] entered again into a synagogue; and a man was there whose hand was withered. They were watching Him to see if He would heal him on the Sabbath, so that they might accuse Him. He said to the man with the withered hand, "Get up and come forward!" And He said to them, "Is it lawful to do good or to do harm on the Sabbath, to save a life or to kill?" But they kept silent.
>
> After looking around at them with anger, grieved at their hardness of heart, He said to the man, "Stretch out your hand." And he stretched it out, and his hand was restored. The Pharisees went out and immediately began

---

[17] Exodus 20:8–11
[18] Mark 2:27–28

conspiring with the Herodians against Him, as to how they might destroy Him.[19]

The Pharisees missed the point. Legalism hardened their hearts to the man with a withered hand. Yet this man wasn't the only one Jesus healed on a Sabbath day. He healed a woman who had endured a sickness for eighteen years, a man suffering from dropsy, and a man ill for thirty-eight years, along with many others.[20]

I think it would be awful to have Jesus look with anger at me if I were to observe the Sabbath with a false sense of piety, believing a day was more important than a person. The apostle Paul, under the inspiration of the Holy Spirit, wrote plainly about the Sabbath and where our focus of worship and devotion should be:

> When you were dead in your transgressions and the uncircumcision of your flesh, He made you alive together with Him, having forgiven us all our transgressions, having canceled out the certificate of debt consisting of decrees against us, which was hostile to us; and He has taken it out of the way, having nailed it to the cross.
>
> When He had disarmed the rulers and authorities, He made a public display of them, having triumphed over them through Him. Therefore no one is to act as your judge in regard to food or drink or in respect to a festival or a new moon or a Sabbath day—things which are a mere shadow of what is to come; but the substance belongs to Christ.[21]

Indeed, *the substance belongs to Christ.* These things cast a mere shadow. Yes, the Sabbath means a full day of rest. Nevertheless, as our Lord pointed out, life still happens.

What is your view of the Sabbath? Are you like the Pharisee, pointing your finger at a brother's spiritual expression of the day as not good enough? Do you neglect a day of rest, renewal, and opportunity to refocus on what matters—your relationship with God?

---

[19] Mark 3:1–6
[20] Luke 13:11-12, 14:2-4, John 5:5-9
[21] Colossians 2:13-17

Take that Sabbath rest. Commit to that one day in seven to rest, taking a blessed opportunity to celebrate your great God through fellowship, prayer, thanksgiving, and family. Experience how this can remarkably improve your life.

So there remains a Sabbath rest for the people of God.
For the one who has entered His rest has himself
also rested from his works, as God did from His.
—HEBREWS 4:9–10

My Task/Challenge

_____

_____

_____

_____

_____

_____

_____

_____

_____

_____

_____

_____

My Outcome/Results

_____

_____

_____

_____

_____

_____

_____

_____

_____

_____

_____

_____

DAY 4 ~ *The Impact of an Eyewitness*

"Only give heed to yourself and keep your soul diligently, so that you do not forget the things which your eyes have seen and they do not depart from your heart all the days of your life; but make them known to your sons and your grandsons."
—DEUTERONOMY 4:9

The word "diligently" stands out for me in the above passage. Merriam-Webster defines the word *diligent* as "characterized by steady, earnest, and energetic effort."[22] Does that sound passive or passionate? I believe the words "earnest" and "energetic" give us the answer. Moses told eyewitnesses to remember the details, the evidence for the events they observed or experienced. God wanted them to recount the details to their children and grandchildren with earnest.

> Now Mount Sinai was all in smoke because the LORD descended upon it in fire; and its smoke ascended like the smoke of a furnace, and the whole mountain quaked violently. When the sound of the trumpet grew louder and louder, Moses spoke and God answered him with thunder.[23]

The passage above refers back to an incident in the wilderness that was up-close and personal. At the prompting of thick clouds, thunder, lightning, fire, and trumpets so loud that the people of Israel trembled as they gathered with great anticipation at the foot of Mount Sinai to meet their God. Shortly after that, God called Moses for a critical meeting. God presented him with the *Decalogue*, more popularly known as *The Ten Commandments*.

The Lord directed Israel to follow the commandments with diligence, and with that same diligence, to remember how they had received them. This event would not be one they would casually pass out of their mind as if it were just an unusual

---

[22] http://www.merriam-webster.com/dictionary/diligent
[23] Exodus 19:18–19

thunderstorm. The meeting with God at Mount Sinai was a partial revealing of God's majesty to them. They witnessed an event to pass on to generations, an overwhelming introduction to God, Himself.

In December 1991, a different eyewitness account impacted my life personally and profoundly, moving me from skeptic to fall-on-my-face believer. In that hotel room in Morgan Hill, California, I read this passage:

> What was from the beginning, what we have heard, what we have seen with our eyes, what we have looked at and touched with our hands, concerning the Word of Life—and the life was manifested, and we have seen and testify and proclaim to you the eternal life, which was with the Father and was manifested to us—what we have seen and heard we proclaim to you also, so that you too may have fellowship with us; and indeed our fellowship is with the Father, and with His Son Jesus Christ. These things we write, so that our joy may be made complete.[24]

The apostle John's eyewitness account and invitation for fellowship with God moved me to total repentance. The eyewitness testimonies throughout Scripture cemented my faith. I realized from the evidence presented during Walter Martin's radio program, not only for the deity of Christ but also for the validity of the Bible, that it was indeed God's Word, and I could, therefore, trust it. It then logically followed that I could believe the eyewitness accounts as well.

I then spent the following year exploring and reading God's Word cover to cover. By April 1993, I shared evidence for Yeshua's resurrection from a small pulpit in Santa Cruz, California. Little did I know what God had planned for my life: a speaking, teaching, and writing ministry just around the corner. Oh, the power of only one eyewitness account!

When we diligently keep within our heart and mind the remarkable works God accomplishes in our lives—like the moment of our salvation—we can passionately share Him with others, especially our children. We bear witness, just as the children of

---

[24] 1 John 1:1–4

Israel saw God in action. We diligently share our faith with our children because when we do not, the spiritual Canaanites develop a higher chance of passing their values, goals, and gods on to them.

What our children as adults do with our testimony falls to them. They alone will stand before God accountable. Thankfully, when we are faithful to His precept in this area, we can stand before God with a clear conscience, no matter what our children choose.

We diligently remember and keep the events in our hearts, in our innermost being, as a dominant part of our memory so we can live pleasing to the God of all glory. Not only can we say, "Look what God has done *for* me," but also, "Look at what God has done *through* me!" What we experience and witness, we can pass on to others.

Have you diligently recounted to people closest to you how God revealed Himself to you through life circumstances? Have you made the acts of God in your life known to your children and grandchildren or others? How about sharing them with the person in a repair shop, in the doctor's waiting room, or the individual in your fellowship who needs encouragement? If you haven't yet, don't miss another opportunity. Determine today that the next time the opportunity presents itself, you will diligently share your faith. Just imagine the impact your diligence can have on the lives of others!

*"You will receive power when the Holy Spirit
has come upon you; and you shall be My witnesses
both in Jerusalem, and in all Judea and Samaria,
and even to the remotest part of the earth."*
—ACTS 1:8

My Task/Challenge

_____
_____
_____
_____
_____
_____
_____
_____
_____
_____
_____

My Outcome/Results

_____
_____
_____
_____
_____
_____
_____
_____
_____
_____
_____

DAY 5 ~ Testy Trials

"You shall remember all the way which the LORD your God has led you in the wilderness these forty years, that He might humble you, testing you, to know what was in your heart, whether you would keep His commandments or not."
—DEUTERONOMY 8:2

The children of Israel didn't travel alone during their wilderness journey. God accompanied them, ultimately providing for them every step of the way. He swallowed up their pursuers in the Red Sea, served manna for breakfast and quail for dinner, lead them with a cloud by day and a pillar of fire by night, poured water from a rock and healing from Moses's staff, and spoke His words of life. The people of God could not boast in self-reliance or their vast resourcefulness. They could only boast in God.

God led His people into a desolate place, away from distractions, enslavements, and Egypt's abundant resources. There He tried, tested, and humbled them with fiery serpents and a terrifying report about the Canaanites[25] as they pitched their tents for forty years. Their response to these trials exposed their hearts, attitudes, and perspectives.

God knows the human heart. The challenge is getting His creatures to understand it too. As we read various accounts throughout Scripture for the first time, we might wonder if, when push comes to shove, the individual God is testing will keep His commands. Although the children of Israel grumbled their way through the wilderness, not all biblical personalities who needed God's grace complained against Him. Not all turned from Him in distrust to create a god of Egypt. Not all accused Him as unfaithful.

Job was indeed a man humbled by trial. However, God did not test Job because He wanted to discover what was truly in Job's heart or even for Job to know his soul. Our omniscient God

---

[25] Numbers 13:32–33

fashioned the trial for Satan to behold Job's response to adversity. Once tried and tested, Job received God's vindication before his "comforters," unlike the unbelieving Israelites. The latter lost their opportunity to enter the Promised Land, for they feared a dreadful report more than they trusted God.

Another man with a physical trial sought healing and, perhaps, an answer to why he suffered from an affliction. He implored the Lord three times to heal his condition. The apostle Paul wrote:

> There was given me a thorn in the flesh, a messenger of Satan to torment me—to keep me from exalting myself! And He has said to me, "My grace is sufficient for you, for power is perfected in weakness."
>
> Most gladly, therefore, I will rather boast about my weaknesses, so that the power of Christ may dwell in me. Therefore I am well content with weaknesses, with insults, with distresses, with persecutions, with difficulties, for Christ's sake; for when I am weak, then I am strong.[26]

When tried and tested, can you confidently say these words with Paul? No one is greater than his master is. I believe Paul embraced that perspective. Our Lord Yeshua, tested by Satan in the wilderness, suffered the horrors of the cross with all its humiliation, yet the words from the depth of His heart spilled out, "Father, forgive them; for they do not know what they are doing."[27] Our Messiah, Jesus, forever exemplifies grace through suffering. There is a reason for pain, a reason for testing, a reason for trials, and after every horrific storm, often a dazzling rainbow appears.

What does the pressure from difficulties produce in you? Do you run to your personal Egypt? Or do you lean hard on a loving God? Do you dial everyone else before calling on the One who allowed the trial, and knows its purpose and outcome? Is prayer your last resort or first thought?

What is your reaction when someone you know passes through a wilderness journey? Are you like one of Job's so-called friends? Do you comfort, or do you automatically assume there

---

[26] 2 Corinthians 12:7–10
[27] Luke 23:34

must be a secret sin in your friend's life? What kind of comforter are you? Do you try to solve the problem?

Sometimes it is best to remain quiet. Job's visitors began that way, silently supporting him in his distress until they opened their mouths. At one time or another, we entertain "comforters" who seem to say to each other before their visit, "Please pass the salt," so that they can rub it into our wounds. Examine how you handle your wilderness journeys, but also how you respond to other people during their times of testing. Ask the Lord for strength, wisdom, and courage to rest, knowing He is God.

> *"Lo, I am with you always, even to the end of the age."*
> —MATTHEW 28:20

My Task/Challenge

My Outcome/Results

DAY 6 ~ *Treasures in Heaven*

"But you shall remember the LORD your God,
For it is He who is giving you power to make wealth."
—DEUTERONOMY 8:18

The passage just before today's opening verse reveals our natural tendency. It underscores why we need to remember that it is the Lord who blesses us with wealth, not ourselves. Otherwise, our proud hearts will declare from our lips, "My power and the strength of my hand made me this wealth."[28] In other words, we think, *God Who?* How easily we forget when all seems to go our way.

Though the passage above relates to the children of Israel remembering when the Lord supplied their needs in the wilderness, I cannot help but remember a certain biblical king who arrogantly admired his kingdom from his palace rooftop.

Earlier in the evening, King Nebuchadnezzar had an unusual dream. Briefly, in the dream, a huge tree was cut down to size. Daniel, the prophet, interpreted for the king that the tree represented Nebuchadnezzar himself and suggested humility would be the king's best course of action.

One year later, the dream and warning long forgotten, Nebuchadnezzar patted himself on the back while gazing upon his glorious kingdom, a reflection of his power—or so he thought. Nebuchadnezzar boldly declared:

"Is this not Babylon the great, which I myself have built as a royal residence by the might of my power and for the glory of my majesty?"[29]

That sounded much like, "My power and the strength of my hand made me this wealth." Indeed, for Nebuchadnezzar, as soon as the words left his mouth, his life would not be the same.

---

[28] Deuteronomy 8:17
[29] Daniel 4:30

Stripped of his glory, for the next seven years, Nebuchadnezzar behaved like a wild animal in the field until he lifted his eyes to heaven and acknowledged the true source of his power and wealth. He finally recognized what Daniel had said. "The Most High is ruler over the realm of mankind and bestows it on whomever He wishes."[30] The result was a freshly humbled king. (Take a moment to read Daniel 4.) Nebuchadnezzar gained a healthy perspective regarding material blessings and the One who bestows them.

On the other hand, wealthy Job did not need a change in fortune to remind him of the true source. Though Job lost everything by worldly standards, he remained the wealthiest man of his time. The proof of his true wealth resided in his words and actions amid his calamity. His wealth was his relationship with God.

The Scriptures reveal upon learning about his great earthly losses, including his children, Job arose, tore his robe, shaved his head, fell to the ground, and worshiped. He said, "Naked I came from my mother's womb, and naked I shall return there. The LORD gave and the LORD has taken away. Blessed be the name of the LORD."[31] What freedom! What maturity! What an example!

Our Lord Jesus also exposed the human heart's attitude regarding wealth in a discussion He had with a rich young ruler. The man asked Yeshua, "Good Teacher, what shall I do to inherit eternal life?"[32] (People always seem to want a list. It sounds easier to check off something as *complete* rather than feel the pinch of self-sacrifice.)

In response, Yeshua suggested, almost as an aside, "One thing you still lack; sell all that you possess and distribute it to the poor, and you shall have treasure in heaven; and come, follow Me."[33]

Jesus offered an awesome invitation. Unfortunately, the wealthy man did not see it that way. The next verse states that the young ruler went away sorrowful. In another account of this same

---

[30] Daniel 4:25
[31] Job 1:20–21
[32] Luke 18:18
[33] Luke 18:22

event, it states that the young man left grieving because he owned much property.[34] How tragic! He clung to his wealth and missed the gift of eternal life.

Then, of course, there was another man of wealth whom Yeshua encountered. This man of small stature, Zacchaeus, a chief tax collector, needed only one incident to change his heart regarding his wealth. This time Yeshua did not invite the wealthy man to follow Him. He invited Himself to Zacchaeus's home for dinner.

Zacchaeus felt so overwhelmed by the prospect of Yeshua's visit that he determined to give half his money to the poor and pay back four times what he appropriated from others. Overflowing joy and gratitude, as well as a true desire for generosity, filled his repentant, grateful heart. It is true that those who are forgiven much, love much.

The wealthy ruler viewed himself as keeping the whole law. He felt he was good enough for God. Yet he never saw his pride, sin, or greed. How tragic. He completely missed the fact that he could not get past the first commandment— "You shall have no other gods before Me"[35]—without breaking it. Ouch!

What is your view of material wealth? Are you clinging to it with clenched fists? Are you grasping for it at the expense of those you love, claiming you are gaining wealth for *them*? Do you boast about it like Nebuchadnezzar? Could you resign yourself to the loss of it like Job? Are you selfish with it like the rich young ruler? Are you a joyful giver like Zacchaeus?

Often, professing believers ask the question, "Do I tithe my income according to the gross or net amount?"

I gently respond, "If you need to ask, perhaps you are not ready to do either because you do not yet view it as an act of worship."

With an open hand, allow the Lord to reveal your heart regarding finances and possessions, never forgetting He is the source and supply. Then be humbled, grateful, and generous.

---

[34] Mark 10:22
[35] Exodus 20:3

"Now I, Nebuchadnezzar, praise, exalt and honor the King of
heaven, for all His works are true and His ways just,
and He is able to humble those who walk in pride."
—DANIEL 4:37

My Task/Challenge

_____
_____
_____
_____
_____
_____
_____
_____
_____
_____
_____
_____

My Outcome/Results

_____
_____
_____
_____
_____
_____
_____
_____
_____
_____
_____
_____

DAY 7 ~ *Redemption's Price and Power*

*"You shall remember that you were
a slave in the land of Egypt,
And the LORD your God redeemed you."*
—DEUTERONOMY 15:15

The focus for Day 2 of this devotional brought our attention to *freedom* from slavery. Today we will concentrate on *redemption* from slavery. Redemption from slavery means not viewing yourself as merely a human "doing," but rather a human "being" with much value and potential. The slave feels worthless, hopeless, and bound to abuse and monotony until someone steps on the scene and redeems him or her, proclaiming, "No more!"

To *redeem* means "to buy back" or "to free from captivity by payment of ransom."[36] Someone pays the price to reclaim a person or possession. Redemption usually costs the redeemer something of value.

With the price of a lamb's blood upon their doorposts, the children of Israel participated in the first Passover meal and then a mass exodus from slavery in Egypt. Moses, during one of his many intercessory moments for Israel, stated:

"I prayed to the LORD and said, 'O Lord God, do not destroy Your people, even Your inheritance, whom You have redeemed through Your greatness, whom You have brought out of Egypt with a mighty hand.'"[37]

The psalmist expressed God's redemption of Israel beautifully:

You are the God who works wonders; You have made known Your strength among the peoples. You have

---

[36] http://www.merriam-webster.com/ dictionary/redeem
[37] Deuteronomy 9:26

32

by Your power redeemed Your people, the sons of Jacob and Joseph.[38]

Again, as we read Scripture, the concept of redemption is sprinkled throughout its pages. We find various laws for redeeming land, redeeming individuals in dire circumstances, like the poor, or redeeming people guilty of offenses against one another. In addition to these examples, we discover a glistening jewel: the beautiful redemption of Ruth by Boaz.

Ruth was a widow and a foreigner with nothing for her future but abject poverty. A Moabitess, she forsook all to follow her impoverished, widowed mother-in-law, Naomi, to Bethlehem. Most daughters-in-law under the same circumstances would, upon the death of their husband, return to their former home and family. Not so with Ruth.

Ruth refused to leave Naomi's side and embraced her mother-in-law's life, including her God. Not only this, but Ruth decided to provide what she could for both of them. Ruth faithfully sought potentially dangerous opportunities to be about the hard work of gleaning in fields where she picked up leftover grain for their pure survival.

Unknown to Ruth, one particular area where she gathered, was in the field of a man who happened to be her legal *kinsman-redeemer*. The kinsman-redeemer was the only man with whom the honor or responsibility lay to intervene for a relative in dire circumstances. Ruth worked in the field of a wealthy man named Boaz, who stepped up to redeem a property and also Ruth. What a change in fortune and future! Boaz redeemed Ruth from a potentially hopeless state. She became the bride of her hero.

Many view the account of Ruth and Boaz as a beautiful picture of our redemption through the Messiah. However, our Redeemer paid a high price with His blood. The apostle Peter explained the cost of our redemption. He wrote:

> You were not redeemed with perishable things like silver or gold from your futile way of life inherited from

---

[38] Psalm 77:14–15

your forefathers, but with precious blood, as of a lamb unblemished and spotless, the blood of Christ.[39]

Jesus paid a price that took away all sin—past, present, and future—for all who desire freedom from serving the adversary of our soul. No one wants to be a slave. However, that was our status apart from Yeshua, Jesus. We needed redemption, and He willingly gave Himself for that purpose.

What overflows from your heart when you think of Yeshua redeeming you at such a high price? Earlier I mentioned that a slave feels worthless, hopeless, and bound to abuse and monotony until someone steps on to the scene to redeem him or her. Look at that prior list. Consider how and why you identified with any of those circumstances when your flesh and Satan enslaved you. Now consider how the Redeemer helped you become the opposite of those descriptions: worthwhile, hopeful, free from abuse, trusting in Him.

Our only response can be utter gratitude. Have you considered what your redemption cost Jesus? Have you thanked Him for paying that price for you? Consider where you would be without His sacrifice, both temporally and eternally. Humbly express heartfelt gratitude for your redeemed life in Him.

Oh give thanks to the LORD, for He is good,
for His lovingkindness is everlasting.
Let the redeemed of the LORD say so,
Whom He has redeemed from the hand of the adversary.
—PSALM 107:1–2

---

[39] 1 Peter 1:18–19

My Task/Challenge

My Outcome/Results

DAY 8 ~ *Our Elders' Wisdom*

"Remember the days of old,
Consider the years of all generations.
Ask your father, and he will inform you,
Your elders, and they will tell you."
—DEUTERONOMY 32:7

When I was in my mid-twenties and living three thousand miles away from my parents' home, my father was involved in an accident at his workplace. The tragedy left one man dead, and my father disabled for the rest of his shortened life. I remember realizing that I did not know my father the way I wanted or needed to.

I knew my father's thoughts philosophically because we engaged in lively debates and discussions during my late teens until I moved to the west coast at age twenty-one. Our talks usually began with him asking me something like, "If you were the god of your own world, what kind of a god would you be, and how would you exact punishment?" Some of our discussions lasted until three o'clock in the morning.

I understood Dad's philosophy, but I knew nothing of his past. As a result, once he returned home from the hospital and could talk, I began calling him on the telephone to ask questions. It surprised me how willing he discussed moments of his life and his parents' lives. I am thankful I took the time to lovingly grill him, as this filled me with peace at his death. My father and I left nothing unsaid. Not all children are as fortunate.

"Ask your father, and he will inform you." On Day 4, we looked at the importance of communicating to our children our eyewitness accounts for what God accomplished in our lives. However, the above verse reminds us of the responsibility to know the past reaches both ways. Children should also approach their parents.

The passage beginning this day's devotion, with its important reminder, is from a line in a song Moses sang to Israel, recounting

God's relationship with them and their relationship with Him. The song expressed many powerful reminders.

This particular reminder encouraged the young to remember the past, learning details from parents and elders who eagerly shared their experiences.

Recounting the past stirs up interesting stories but also teaches children the wisdom gained from someone who *has been there.* Remembering the past influences our direction today and in the future—in a positive way if we learn or in a negative way if we do not. After sharing this song, Moses said, "It is not an idle word for you; indeed it is your life."[40] In other words, this song was not a meaningless chant, but rather something to follow. Lives depended upon knowing the past and learning from it.

I wish more people in our culture interviewed their parents. Perhaps an unfortunate lack of respect keeps many young people from interacting with their elders. Perhaps they imagine listening to the older generation as dull or intolerable; perhaps they believe their elders are out of touch. Unfortunately, too many young people believe this to their peril, especially if they dismiss those who have lived long in their walk with the Lord.

In the Old Covenant, a young king held a dangerous, dismissive view of his elders. Rehoboam, son of King Solomon, needed counsel and received it. (Solomon was the wisest man who ever lived, yet Rehoboam witnessed his father living with perpetual compromise. Could this be the reason for the son's lack of respect and disregard for wise counsel from his elders? After Solomon died, Rehoboam became king. The drama played out in 1 Kings 12. Take a moment to read that chapter.)

Rehoboam asked the elders how he should treat the people. They gave sensible advice, yet "he forsook the advice of the elders, which they had given him, and he spoke to them according to the advice of the young men."[41] Rehoboam decided to treat the people harshly; thus, the kingdom summarily divided. The young king could not accept the elders' direction. Instead, he listened to his peers—to the horror of the people.

---

[40] Deuteronomy 32:47
[41] 1 Kings 12:13–14

In Rehoboam's case, his father had passed on, yet he still had elders with the ability to speak wisdom into his life. In the New Testament, a young pastor named Timothy entered the Lord's service. Scripture does not identify Timothy's father, but we do learn that he exemplified strong faith throughout his young life. Who received the praise from Rabbi Paul for Timothy's early spiritual education? His grandmother, Lois, and his mother, Eunice.[42] Timothy listened to and learned from them.

Likewise, God places people in our lives to help us in the maturing process. We can talk to our parents and others about their experiences with God's faithfulness and power. We can learn from their mistakes and God's response to their sins. Do you know more about your parents' partying past than their encounters with a faithful God? If your parents died today, what would you regret not knowing about them? Do you know how God revealed Himself in their lives?

Perhaps your parents are not strong witnesses for the Lord. Find an elder, someone older than you. Contact someone who has walked with the Lord for many years, someone willing to share. As you meet together, bring a pen and paper (or a recorder) to preserve their experiences. Then learn from them. Look at your life for similarities and how you could respond based upon what they teach you. Wisdom is a gift the older generation gives to the younger, and by the Lord's instruction, it is a gift worthy of pursuit.

Hear, O sons, the instruction of a father,
And give attention that you may gain understanding,
For I give you sound teaching; Do not abandon my instruction.
—PROVERBS 4:1–2

---

[42] 2 Timothy 1:5

My Task/Challenge

_____
_____
_____
_____
_____
_____
_____
_____
_____
_____
_____

My Outcome/Results

_____
_____
_____
_____
_____
_____
_____
_____
_____
_____
_____

DAY 9 ~ *Meditations Or Passing Thoughts*

"This book of the law shall not depart from your mouth,
but you shall meditate on it day and night,
so that you may be careful to do according to all that is written in
it; for then you will make your way prosperous,
and then you will have success."
—JOSHUA 1:8

efore Israel entered the Promised Land, God assured Joshua, the nation's new leader, that He would never leave or forsake him. Success would logically follow if Joshua meditated upon God's Word as a way of life. Joshua's way would prosper, including a victory over his enemies. Staying in God's Word would afford him a proper perspective and reward.

Joshua was to meditate upon all revealed Scripture, the Book of the Law. He was not simply to parrot it to the people or peruse it to pass the time until the enemy's wall fell, but to meditate on and *do* the law—to live consistently with what he read.

During King Josiah's reign, thoughtful contemplation upon Scripture changed a nation. After years of neglect, someone found the Book of the Law, dusted it off, and brought it to King Josiah, who had ruled in Judah since he was only eight years old. Yet young Josiah internalized what his elders read.

Josiah's thoughtfulness regarding the Scriptures produced radical changes during his monarchy. His life became his witness. Josiah purged his kingdom of idolatry, cultic practices, and the individuals who engaged in them. Of Josiah, God's Word declared:

> Before him there was no king like him who turned to the LORD with all his heart and with all his soul and with all his might, according to all the law of Moses; nor did any like him arise after him.[43]

---

[43] 2 Kings 23:25

God's Word is an authoritative tool against the enemy of our soul. The writer of Hebrews declared:

> The word of God is living and active and sharper than any two-edged sword, and piercing as far as the division of soul and spirit, of both joints and marrow, and able to judge the thoughts and intentions of the heart.[44]

Keep in mind that Jesus quoted Scripture during his forty days of temptation in the wilderness. Repeatedly, our Lord Yeshua answered the devil's temptations with, "It is written . . ."[45] Yeshua answered with the revealed, written Word of God and "extinguish[ed] the flaming arrows of the evil one."[46]

God's Word is powerful. Satan could not continue pressing temptation upon Jesus. Once Jesus quoted Scripture, that snake in the grass could only move on to a different temptation. Eventually, he gave up altogether until "an opportune time,"[47] which proves that old serpent never really gives up.

Since Satan never gives up entirely, we should diligently meditate upon God's Word. Then, like Jesus, we can quote it aloud when tempted. Satan always manipulates God's Word to serve his purpose, yet we learn from Yeshua that, when used in proper context, the two-edged sword cuts arguments and temptations to shreds.

Meditating upon God's Word involves being quiet, staying still. Many twenty-first-century individuals know little about stillness before the Lord. I hear well-meaning believers say, "My quiet time is when I drive. That's my prayer time." Doing other things while focusing on the Lord, and His Word is not meditating. It is multitasking.

I once saw a book in a Christian bookstore entitled *One Minute Meditations*. However, one minute is not meditation. It is a passing thought! Meditating on the whole counsel of God does not mean giving it a passing thought. Surely, God deserves more from

---

[44] Hebrews 4:12
[45] Matthew 4:4, 7, 10
[46] Ephesians 6:11–18 reveals our battle attire to defeat the enemy.
[47] Luke 4:13

us than that. The Book of the Law is the key to a successful life. Josiah applied it to his life and kingdom, as did Joshua in the Promised Land.

Meditating on God's Word benefits us too. What comes to mind when you hear the word *meditate*? Many people think of transcendental meditation or another mode of mysticism. Or perhaps they envision a young pupil daydreaming during class, staring blank-faced out of the window.

In contrast, biblical meditation is not passive. It is not clearing your mind; it is not for the empty-headed. Biblical meditation is active, combining the mind and soul. It involves thoughtfulness toward God's Word and will and thankfulness for who He is and what He has done. Since meditation is internal and personal, it changes us from the inside out. It is quiet and private, with only God as our companion.

How precious is God's Word to you? How much time do you spend on it? Do you know the whole counsel of God, reading it cover to cover? How would daily meditation upon His Word influence your life right now?

Make the change. Commit to getting up earlier than usual to spend time alone with Him. Commit to ending your day with His Word on your mind. Remember, the beginning verse for today specified "day and night."

God desires to walk with us as He did with Adam. Allow Him to speak His will through His Word, and then obey. You will experience success as the Holy Spirit brings to mind Scripture verses powerful for thwarting temptation, making an important life decision, encouraging a believer, or leading a lost soul into His glorious kingdom.

"Sanctify them in the truth;
Your word is truth."
—JOHN 17:17

My Task/Challenge

_____
_____
_____
_____
_____
_____
_____
_____
_____
_____
_____

My Outcome/Results

_____
_____
_____
_____
_____
_____
_____
_____
_____
_____
_____

DAY 10 ~ *To Die is Gain*

*"Remember now, O LORD, I beseech You,
how I have walked before You in truth and
with a whole heart and have done what is
good in Your sight." And Hezekiah wept bitterly.*
—2 KINGS 20:3

Throughout this devotional, the verse that begins each day with an admonition to remember concerns the prompting of the *reader's* memory. However, today's verse is different. King Hezekiah, understanding that he was gravely ill, petitioned God to remember his good deeds and therefore grant him more years. Essentially, he argued, "I've done so much good; you owe me one, God!"

God permitted the king's self-consumed request, and Hezekiah received fifteen more years of life. During those extended years he begat Manasseh, of whom the Scriptures reveal:

> For he rebuilt the high places which Hezekiah his father had destroyed; and he erected altars for Baal and made an Asherah, as Ahab king of Israel had done, and worshiped all the host of heaven and served them. He built altars in the house of the Lord . . . He made his son pass through the fire, practiced witchcraft and used divination, and dealt with mediums and spiritists. He did much evil in the sight of the Lord provoking Him to anger.[48]

The Scriptures also state that King Manasseh "shed very much innocent blood until he had filled Jerusalem from one end to another."[49]

Eventually, the treasures of the house of God, which Hezekiah proudly showed off after his miraculous recovery, were carried

---

[48] 2 Kings 21:3–6
[49] 2 Kings 21:16

44

away along with the people into Babylonian captivity. Hezekiah could have trusted in the Lord's timing. Instead, he pleaded based upon his perceived goodness and did not lean on God's sovereign will.

What an object lesson for those who desperately want to avoid the inevitable! Aren't the Lord's will and timing better than ours? If we walk with the Lord in the purity of heart and deed, we can welcome death. It means we will see Him, whom we love, face-to-face. Indeed, we can trust His will and wisdom to use difficulty for His glory.

There is no sin in asking for the cup of suffering and death to pass us. Our Lord Jesus made this request. However, He carried the weight and guilt of the world's sins upon Himself. His sweat was tinged with blood, a condition known as hematidrosis. His anguish was so great, Yeshua prayed to the Father in the garden that fateful night, "My Father, if it is possible, let this cup pass from Me; yet not as I will, but as You will."[50] Since it was not possible to redeem fallen humanity apart from the suffering and death of the perfect Passover Lamb, the answer had to be, "It is not possible."

To be sure, the only criteria for every petition we bring before God must be not our will, but His. That is, we must come trusting in God for a better plan. John, the apostle, wrote, "This is the confidence which we have before Him, that, if we ask anything according to His will, He hears us."[51] This rule governs all our requests, including miraculous healing from the brink of death. It must be according to God's will.

The apostle Paul stated one of the healthiest views toward God's will as it related to death. He told the Philippians:

> For to me, to live is Christ and to die is gain. But if I am to live on in the flesh, this will mean fruitful labor for me; and I do not know which to choose. But I am hard-pressed from both directions, having the desire to depart and be with Christ, for that is very much better; yet to remain on in the flesh is more necessary for your sake.[52]

---

[50] Matthew 26:39
[51] 1 John 5:14
[52] Philippians 1:21–24

To the Corinthians, Paul cited a passage from Hosea: "O death, where is your victory? O death, where is your sting?"[53] The sting of death is reserved for those who deny it will happen. As a volunteer EMT and firefighter, I have often seen that individuals who visit the recreational district where I live and serve never imagined it might be their last day. Their belongings reveal that they expected to enjoy the parks, the lakes, and the hiking trails, a journey to the top of Mount Saint Helens or trips through the lava tubes. They do not plan a day trip as if their life would be required of them.

Every person who hit an elk while riding a motorcycle, collided with a drunk driver around a sharp turn, took a header into a speedboat with a WaveRunner, or had a massive heart attack settling into a cabin, had no idea it would be their last day. They had no time to repent and confess their sins before a holy God, whom they met in an instant. It is tragic but true. Many individuals believe they can simply slide into heaven during the last minute, deathbed conversion, so they can ignore the Lord throughout their lives and enjoy the fruit of sin for a season.

What is your attitude regarding death? Do you cling to this life so much that you fear death? Or, is "O death, where is your victory? O death, where is your sting?"[54] your anthem, along with the apostle Paul? Are you storing your reward and treasures in heaven as you look forward to knowing what they are? Do you long to see Him face-to-face? If not, why not?

The more we invest in this life, the harder it will be to leave it. Imagine if, every night, as your head hit the pillow, you believed in the morning you would wake in God's presence. Is there something you need to settle with Him first? It is healthy to consider these matters daily. It allows for self-examination and a changed life before Him.

Unless God translates you into heaven through the Rapture, you will eventually face the moment of your death. Let go of the things you cling to in this life, "and the peace of God, which surpasses all comprehension, will guard your hearts and your minds

---

[53] 1 Corinthians 15:55
[54] 1 Corinthians 15:55

in Christ Jesus."[55] If you trust Him with your life, if you trust Him with your eternity, you can trust Him with the timing and manner of your transition into Glory.

> *A good name is better than a good ointment,*
> *And the day of one's death is*
> *better than the day of one's birth.*
> —ECCLESIASTES 7:1

---

[55] Philippians 4:7

My Task/Challenge

_____
_____
_____
_____
_____
_____
_____
_____
_____
_____
_____

My Outcome/Results

_____
_____
_____
_____
_____
_____
_____
_____
_____
_____
_____

DAY 11 ~ *Facing Fear*

*"Do not be afraid of them; remember the Lord
who is great and awesome."*
—NEHEMIAH 4:14

*F*ear can be a paralyzing emotion—so paralyzing it almost halted the rebuilding of the wall around Jerusalem until Nehemiah stepped in to remind the faithful builders of God's greatness with the words above. A focus on the greatness of God is always the perfect antidote for fear.

What is the source of our strength? To whom can we turn when the going gets tough, and the attacks seem almost too impossible to endure? Whom can we rely upon when the enemy surrounds us? A man named Shammah knew. He would not give a hill of beans—literally—to the Philistines. The entire biblical account is outlined in only two verses:

> Now after him [Eleazar, one of three mighty men who joined David in battle] was Shammah the son of Agee a Hararite. And the Philistines were gathered into a troop where there was a plot of ground full of lentils, and the people fled from the Philistines. But he took his stand in the midst of the plot, defended it and struck the Philistines; and the LORD brought about a great victory.[56]

Perhaps discouraging voices were yelling to him, "Come on, Shammah, forget that insignificant plot of lentils and run for your life with the rest of us!" I can just imagine what that scene was like as one man struck relentlessly at his enemy. Did you notice it was *the Lord* who brought about a great victory? Shammah was simply His faithful vehicle.

Sometimes we can feel like Shammah taking a stand where no one else will with perhaps voices calling us to give up because the task seems impossible. I remember those times through the years

---

[56] 2 Samuel 23:11–12

when my husband and I heard such voices concerning particular parenting decisions, which, in retrospect, we are very thankful we made. When the results were in, we did appreciate the kudos we got for hanging in there. As an example, especially from those who at first snickered at our decision to home-educate our kids. What was essential for us was that we based our conclusions upon God's Word and His will for us as parents and servants. No doubt about it, the "Philistines" did not like our way of life. Nevertheless, we continued to stand our ground, trusting not in our ability as parents or servants but the Lord. No wisdom, or strength, or success of battle happens without His loving intervention and reliance upon His Word.

Remember the words of our Lord, who said:

> "But beware of men, for they will hand you over to the courts and scourge you in their synagogues; and you will even be brought before governors and kings for My sake, as a testimony to them and to the Gentiles. But when they hand you over, do not worry about how or what you are to say; for it will be given you in that hour what you are to say. For it is not you who speak, but it is the Spirit of your Father who speaks in you."[57]

A man born blind knew this reality. Yeshua, Jesus, restored his sight. Shortly afterward, influential leaders of the Jewish people confronted him. The Pharisees threatened that if he did not tell them what they wanted to hear, they would toss him out of the synagogue, meaning a severing from his people and his God. Yet, filled with boldness when cross-examined for the second time concerning his miraculous healing, his response hinted at what Yeshua meant by having the right words for the moment. I love this bold exchange:

> They [the Pharisees] reviled him [the blind man] and said, "You are His disciple, but we are disciples of Moses. We know that God has spoken to Moses, but as for this man, we do not know where He is from."
>
> The man answered and said to them, "Well, here is an amazing thing, that you do not know where He is

---

[57] Matthew 10:17–20

from, and yet He opened my eyes. We know that God does not hear sinners; but if anyone is God-fearing and does His will, He hears him. Since the beginning of time it has never been heard that anyone opened the eyes of a person born blind. If this man were not from God, He could do nothing."

They answered him, "You were born entirely in sins, and are you teaching us?" So they put him out.

Jesus heard that they had put him out, and finding him, He said, "Do you believe in the Son of Man?"

He answered, "Who is He, Lord, that I may believe in Him?"

Jesus said to him, "You have both seen Him, and He is the one who is talking with you."

And he said, "Lord, I believe." And he worshiped Him.

This man went directly from the cruel rejection of the Pharisees into the arms of the Lord. That is the perfect place to be!

Do naysayers afflict your life? Are there folks who want you to doubt God's greatness? Do you allow the Holy Spirit to give you boldness when confronted? Is fear preventing you from all you can be or do for the Lord? Do you lack the confidence of the blind man?

Fear makes us do foolish, impulsive things, or stops us in our tracks when we should move forward. When fear fills your heart, it is proof that faith does not. Confront your fear. Confess your fear. Then obey the prompting of the Holy Spirit to step forward when He calls you. Do not put off any longer what you delayed due to fear. Trust in Him, and He will bring about a victory!

*For God did not give us a spirit of timidity
(of cowardice, of craven and cringing and fawning fear),
but [He has given us a spirit] of power and of love
and of calm and well-balanced mind and discipline and self-control.*
—2 TIMOTHY 1:7, AMP

My Task/Challenge

_____
_____
_____
_____
_____
_____
_____
_____
_____
_____

My Outcome/Results

_____
_____
_____
_____
_____
_____
_____
_____
_____
_____

DAY 12 ~ *The Weight of Guilt*

*"They refused to listen, and did not remember Your wondrous deeds
which You had performed among them; so they became stubborn
and appointed a leader to return to their slavery in Egypt.
But You are a God of forgiveness, gracious and compassionate,
slow to anger and abounding in lovingkindness;
and You did not forsake them."*
—NEHEMIAH 9:17

With the rebuilding of the walls surrounding Jerusalem in 445 BC, a great assembly gathered. The Book of the Law was read aloud, people repented of their sins, and prayer once again recounted God's fidelity toward Israel. The prayer also expressed a painful reminder of how, after God led the children of Israel out of Egyptian bondage, they forsook Him. They built a golden calf, claiming *it* had rescued them instead of the hand of the Lord. How did this happen?

Impatience and resenting their temporal circumstances developed a desire in them to go back to Egypt. Lack of faith and arrogant, misguided confidence in their self-reliance lured them toward their old bondage. A stiff neck and deaf ear to the Lord's clear will, along with a short memory, can yield dire consequences. The worst thing the children of Israel could have done was return to slavery in Egypt. Their glorious God knew this. All too often, when we refuse the Lord's clear guidance, feel the weight of our consequences, and seek Him for mercy, we replay Israel's history.

When we ask God for forgiveness, we know He holds the cure for our burdened soul. King David realized this when he misguidedly commanded a census. The great commander Joab implored David not to count the people against the will of God. All King David's commanders urged him in the same manner. Nevertheless, David ignored Joab and the others, ordering him to count the people. After almost ten months, David received the number and responded with regret:

Now David's heart troubled him after he had numbered the people. So David said to the LORD, "I have sinned greatly in what I have done. But now, O LORD, please take away the iniquity of Your servant, for I have acted very foolishly."[58]

David admitted to playing the fool, and God did not spare the rod of correction. In an unusual exchange, the Lord gave David his choice of penalty. The consequence for David's decision to disobey the Lord was that the number of people he counted significantly diminished due to a divinely inflicted plague. Though David received forgiveness from the Lord, he still endured the earthly consequence of his sin. Unfortunately, so did the people.

While King David in the Old Covenant refused to listen to wise and godly counsel, in the New Covenant, the disciple Peter just plain forgot Jesus's warning regarding his denial—times three. The book of Matthew records the exchange between Yeshua and Peter after our Lord warned the disciples of His imminent death—and that they would thereafter scatter.

But Peter said to Him, "Even though all may fall away because of You, I will never fall away."

Jesus said to him, "Truly I say to you that this very night, before a rooster crows, you will deny Me three times."

Peter said to Him, "Even if I have to die with You, I will not deny You." All the disciples said the same thing too.[59]

It did not take long. Just hours later, Peter not only denied Jesus but cursed to emphasize his point. When the rooster crowed, the Lord's words crashed upon Peter, along with the weight of his guilt and shame. Scripture reveals that "he went out and wept bitterly."[60] Peter felt the full pressure and consequence of his sin. All who heard him boast earlier could thereafter remind him of this failure.

---

[58] 2 Samuel 24:10
[59] Matthew 26:33–35
[60] Luke 22:62

The good news is that after Peter's mournful repentance and Jesus' resurrection, the Lord forgave and fully restored him. Later, Peter, filled with the Holy Spirit, preached on the day of Pentecost as three thousand people gave their lives to the Lord.

How do you respond when you feel the weight of your guilt? What is your reaction when you violate the Lord's clear Word? Do you try to justify the action? Do you deny everything and anything? Do you blame someone else for your failure?

The best response is to face it, confess it, and accept the consequences. Allow Him to use those consequences to minister to others as He fully restores your soul. The Lord continued to use David, a man after His own heart. He used Peter mightily to build the kingdom, and He can certainly use you. Examine your heart in this area and allow the Lord to show you what you need to see. "If we confess our sins, He is faithful and righteous to forgive us our sins and to cleanse us from all unrighteousness."[61] He will then use you for His glory in a specific and unique way.

It is a trustworthy statement: For if we died with Him,
we will also live with Him; if we endure,
we will also reign with Him; if we deny Him,
He also will deny us; if we are faithless,
He remains faithful, for He cannot deny Himself.
—2 TIMOTHY 2:11–13

---

[61] 1 John 1:9

My Task/Challenge

_____

_____

_____

_____

_____

_____

_____

_____

_____

_____

_____

My Outcome/Results

_____

_____

_____

_____

_____

_____

_____

_____

_____

_____

_____

DAY 13 ~ Divine Design

When I consider Your heavens, the work of Your fingers,
The moon and the stars, which You have ordained;
What is man that You take thought of him,
And the son of man that You care for him?
—PSALM 8:3–4

---

avid the shepherd appreciated the wonder of God's creation. He beheld it with incredible awe. David not only glorified God through His creation but also remembered humanity's place concerning that creation. He wrote:

> By the word of the LORD the heavens were made,
> And by the breath of His mouth all their host.
> He gathers the waters of the sea together as a heap;
> He lays up the deeps in storehouses.
> Let all the earth fear the LORD;
> Let all the inhabitants of the world stand in awe of Him.[62]

We certainly "stand in awe" of what we see and learn from creation. We recognize God's incredible power, imagination, beauty, and love for humanity. Heavenly bodies help us acknowledge our Maker and glorify Him because "day to day pours forth speech, and night to night reveals knowledge."[63]

Those words came alive for me one evening through my son, Mikael. It had been a particularly long and busy day. Mikael sprang into his bed, slipped under his thick comforter, looked at me with his big green eyes, and said, "Lay with me?" He was eight years old and was to be baptized the following weekend. As I lay next to him, holding his soft little face in my hands, he made a rather startling confession.

---

[62] Psalm 33:6–8
[63] Psalm 19:2

57

"You know, Mom, when I was really little, I mean really little, I used to sneak out of my bedroom and sit in front of the slider in the middle of the night when everyone was asleep. I would sit there and look up at the stars, and it was like someone was saying to me, 'There's another place, there's another place.'"

I asked, "A better place?"

"Yes, yes," he said so excitedly he seemed about to burst, "a better place!" With a heavy sigh and a relieved tone like someone who has found the true meaning of life, he proclaimed, "And then you told me about heaven, and I said to myself, 'That's it, that's the other place, the better place!'" There it was, the eternal beckoning of God to an eight-year-old boy gazing with wonder upon heavenly bodies.

The prophet Isaiah wrote:

> For thus says the LORD, who created the heavens (He is the God who formed the earth and made it, He established it and did not create it a waste place, but formed it to be inhabited), "I am the Lord, and there is none else."[64]

Did you catch that? God did not create the earth a waste place but *formed it to be inhabited*, and for Him, those inhabitants are of tremendous worth.

With the vast array of planets astronomers find, upon further inspection, they realize these bodies are waste places with our humble abode the exception. Their discovery prompts me to consider the *Anthropic Principle*. This heady-sounding principle proposes that each of the seemingly random laws and constants in physics, all of which impact the basic structure of the universe, are not random at all. In fact, these are the exact values needed for a universe capable of sustaining not only life in general but human life on our planet, specifically. Everything from the thickness of the earth's crust, the gravitational force of the earth, the distance of the sun, the rotation of the earth and its axial tilt, the speed of light,

---

[64] Isaiah 45:18

and the distance between stars in the galaxy are precise and necessary for human life on earth.[65]

The universe, created by an intelligent Designer, is fine-tuned for our existence. Our planet is not a *waste place*. Instead, it is inhabited by beings made in God's image, whom He loves to beckon with a whisper to the soul, "There's another place, a better place." Moreover, that place is in the presence of our Creator. The Apostle John's opening statement from his Gospel reads:

> In the beginning was the Word, and the Word was with God, and the Word was God. He was in the beginning with God. All things came into being through Him, and apart from Him nothing came into being that has come into being.[66]

When we read that passage further, we realize *He* refers to Jesus. By Him, all things came into being. He is our Creator. He is our Sustainer. The writer of Hebrews states that:

> God, after He spoke long ago to the fathers in the prophets in many portions and in many ways, in these last days has spoken to us in His Son, whom He appointed heir of all things, through whom also He made the world. And He is the radiance of His glory and the exact representation of His nature, and upholds all things by the word of His power.[67]

As I search for an answer, it seems gravity does not have an explanation for its source. Scientists can explain gravity's effects and with calculations its impact, but not where it originated. Yet the above passage explains it quite nicely. *He upholds all things by the word of His power*. It is a divine, "Don't move." And yet, His Word reveals that one day it will all change and become more glorious than we can imagine.

When was the last time you stargazed, walked through the woods, or took a hike in the quietness of God's creation? The Lord

---

[65] For more information on the anthropic principle, please see Norman L. Geisler, *Baker Encyclopedia of Christian Apologetics* (Grand Rapids, MI Baker Books, 1999).
[66] John 1:1–3
[67] Hebrews 1:1–3

speaks powerfully in a quiet environment. Yes, He gets our attention through the earthquake, the tsunami, and the twister. However, once He captures our attention, once we drop the cell phone, turn off the video games, or set aside the remote control, He speaks. Because He often speaks subtly to the soul, it makes sense to get quiet. If He can speak to an eight-year-old boy's heart or a young shepherd with his flock, He can certainly speak to yours.

Are you quiet enough to listen? Take time today, no matter your schedule, to seek Him through the stillness and beauty of His creation.

Then I saw a new heaven and a new earth; for the first heaven and the first earth passed away, and there is no longer any sea.
And I saw the holy city, new Jerusalem,
coming down out of heaven from God,
made ready as a bride adorned for her husband . . .
And He who sits on the throne said,
"Behold, I am making all things new."
—REVELATION 21:1–2, 5

My Task/Challenge

_____

_____

_____

_____

_____

_____

_____

_____

_____

_____

_____

My Outcome/Results

_____

_____

_____

_____

_____

_____

_____

_____

_____

_____

_____

DAY 14 ~ *The Joy of Fellowship*

*From You comes my praise in the great assembly; I shall pay my
vows before those who fear Him.
The afflicted will eat and be satisfied;
Those who seek Him will praise the Lord. Let your heart live forever!
All the ends of the earth will remember and turn to the Lord,
And all the families of the nations will worship before You.*
—PSALM 22:25-27

---

oday's passage above causes me to imagine the Feast of
Tabernacles or *Sukkot*, found first in Leviticus 23:33–44.
Take a moment to read the entire passage. In verses 40–44
below, we read:

"Now on the first day you shall take for yourselves
the foliage of beautiful trees, palm branches and boughs
of leafy trees and willows of the brook, and you shall
rejoice before the LORD your God for seven days. You
shall thus celebrate it as a feast to the LORD for seven days
in the year.

"It shall be a perpetual statute throughout your
generations; you shall celebrate it in the seventh month.
You shall live in booths for seven days; all the native-born
in Israel shall live in booths, so that your generations may
know that I had the sons of Israel live in booths when I
brought them out from the land of Egypt. I am the LORD
your God."

In Deuteronomy 16:13–15, we read:

"You shall celebrate [Sukkot] seven days after you
have gathered in from your threshing floor and your wine
vat; and you shall rejoice in your feast, you and your son
and your daughter and your male and female servants
and the Levite and the stranger and the orphan and the
widow who are in your towns.

"Seven days you shall celebrate a feast to the LORD your God in the place which the LORD chooses, because the LORD your God will bless you in all your produce and in all the work of your hands, so that you will be altogether joyful."

The Lord's goal for the children of Israel through this festival was that they be "altogether joyful." Now, I don't know about you, but growing up in the tradition I did, I was not left with a view of a God Whose great desire was that I should *be altogether joyful*. My inaccurate, misguided view of God was that He was waiting for me to mess up so He could flick me off to hell. That is quite far from the real character of God. In my former tradition, I never knew fellowship with other individuals who were filled with the Holy Spirit, whose favorite subject was Jesus, the Messiah of Israel.

What a beautiful celebration Sukkot is! It is joyful, and with the reading of God's Word, it is also an excellent time to reflect on His bounty and blessings, and of course, a time to celebrate with many others while expressing a heart of true thanksgiving to the One who made it all possible. I think the overflow of emotion during this celebration, felt by people who truly understand God's heart in giving His people this type of festival, is proof that turning to the Lord—remembering Him—prompts an attitude of joyful worship.

The call to be joyful in the assembly inspires me to believe we should celebrate whenever we fellowship with the saints. The apostle Paul in Philippians implores his audience to "Rejoice in the Lord always; again I will say, rejoice! Let your gentle spirit be known to all men. The Lord is near."[68]

We are to rejoice not merely for a weeklong celebration, but always. Yet, do we? Are we rejoicing in our fellowship with each other? We had better get accustomed to celebrating together, especially considering this prophecy in Zechariah: "Then it will come about that any who are left of all the nations that went

[68] Philippians 4:4–5

against Jerusalem will go up from year to year to worship the king, the LORD of hosts, and to celebrate"—to celebrate what? Sukkot.[69]

In the book of Revelation as the New Jerusalem comes down from heaven, we read:

> And I heard a loud voice from the throne, saying, "Behold, the tabernacle of God is among men, and He will dwell among them, and they shall be His people, and God Himself will be among them."[70]

God, Himself, will tabernacle among us. The passage also states that the nations will come into the Holy City. What a beautiful picture—God among His people in unhindered fellowship and we among each other in joy-filled solidarity.

Isn't it remarkable how everyone wants some form of world peace? Everyone seems to be longing for Utopia, marked by unbridled joy. It's interesting to me that today's opening verse comes at the end of a psalm that gives a perfect depiction of the crucifixion. Only after the crucifixion and resurrection can restoration be accomplished. World peace cannot happen apart from Yeshua's sacrificial death, His resurrection, and His coming in-person to restore it all at the appointed time.

Until that blessed day of newness in heaven and on earth, God the Holy Spirit tabernacles in the hearts of individuals who choose to worship God in Spirit and truth. Because of this, we should rejoice together in all things, always.

Do you have that attitude when you are among God's people? Are you a sweet fragrance in the assembly, or are you a faultfinder? Since we do not know the time of the restoration to come, why not practice peace right now, with those individuals among your fellowship? Is there someone you find fault with who you would rather not be with for all eternity? You need a heart and attitude adjustment. Are you following the command to rejoice always? If not, make a concerted effort this day to let go of whatever is depressing your joy.

---

[69] Zechariah 14:16
[70] Revelation 21:3

Pray for a change in focus and attitude. Then allow God to fill you with inexpressible joy, and genuine love for your family in Christ. You will be thankful you did, and so will those of your assembly.

Finally, brethren, rejoice, be made complete,
be comforted, be like-minded, live in peace;
and the God of love and peace will be with you.
—2 CORINTHIANS 13:11

My Task/Challenge

_____

_____

_____

_____

_____

_____

_____

_____

_____

My Outcome/Results

_____

_____

_____

_____

_____

_____

_____

_____

_____

DAY 15 ~ *Peacefully Sleeping*

When I remember You on my bed,
I meditate on You in the night watches, for You have been my help,
and in the shadow of Your wings I sing for joy.
—PSALM 63:6–7

In the lead up to a fateful night in Babylon, the captive Daniel awaited his promotion to the highest position of honor in the kingdom. However, jealousy also reigned in that kingdom ruled by Darius the Mede. One hundred twenty-two officials plotted together to find some accusation against Daniel to mark him for permanent disposal.

> Then the commissioners and satraps began trying to find a ground of accusation against Daniel in regard to government affairs; but they could find no ground of accusation or evidence of corruption, inasmuch as he was faithful, and no negligence or corruption was to be found in him. Then these men said, "We will not find any ground of accusation against this Daniel unless we find it against him with regard to the law of his God."[71]

The officials found no earthly accusation against Daniel, so they decided to trap him by way of his spiritual faithfulness. They plotted, then enticed King Darius through an elevation of his ego to sign a decree they knew Daniel would have to violate: a decree declaring that there would be no worship of anyone or anything except the king himself. Darius's desire to elevate himself backfired when his favored advisor continued to pray, as the officials knew he would, to the true God of heaven and earth. Darius, realizing he could not break his permanent injunction, escorted Daniel to the lion's den and certain death.

It was a long, sleepless, excruciating night for Darius. For Daniel, however, it was a restful night of trusting God with the outcome. Perhaps Daniel tucked himself comfortably against the

---

[71] Daniel 6:4–5

lion's soft fur, meditating upon God's Word, singing a few praise songs, lions tapping their paws to the beat, knowing the Lord was and always would be his help.

King Darius, on the other hand, had no such comfort. The words *What have I done?* ran through his tortured mind. At dawn, Darius rushed to the lion's den to find a well-rested, confident, faithful servant of the living God alive and well. Out came Daniel, completely unharmed, with testimony on his lips of how the Lord had shut the lion's mouth.

Notice the Lord did not slay the lions to save Daniel's life. No, they would soon serve their purpose. As Daniel confidently strode out of the den, in his false accusers were then escorted. Payday, someday. Psalm 37 states, "The wicked plots against the righteous and gnashes at him with his teeth. The Lord laughs at him, for He sees his day is coming."[72]

True, unbridled trust in the living God produces a faith so great that sleep will not evade the one who trusts no matter what the circumstances. In Acts 12, we see another man whose confidence in his Lord prompted the ability to sleep in another type of den: this time, a cell.

The apostle Peter found himself arrested and tossed into prison with four squads of soldiers to guard him. Peter knew this was not the most ideal of situations. Herod had just put James, John's brother, "to death with the sword."[73] Peter realized he would soon face the same fate.

As his brothers and sisters in the Lord prayed, Peter freaked out. He screamed and yelled, "No, no! I don't want to die! Get me outta this miserable prison!"

Well, that might be how we would imagine the outcome. Actually, the passage states, "On the very night when Herod was about to bring him forward, Peter was sleeping between two soldiers, bound with two chains, and guards in front of the door were watching over the prison."[74]

---

[72] Psalm 37:12–13
[73] Acts 12:2
[74] Acts 12:6

Peter slept. At dawn, the plan was to bring him before Herod to face the sword, yet Peter slept soundly. So soundly, in fact, that when the angel came to free him from the prison, Peter had to be nudged awake. Talk about peaceful trust! Then again, the Lord Yeshua was his example. Peter was an eyewitness as Jesus slept soundly in the sea-tossed vessel to the fear and amazement of all His disciples.[75]

God was in control, so *Peter slept soundly.* The funny thing about this account is that the ones who were distressed were the saints who prayed for his rescue. They were the ones who lacked faith in Rhoda's proclamation that Peter was free from his chains, at their gate, and eager to prove to them that God heard their prayers.

Both Daniel and Peter could be accused of nothing but staying true to God. Are you free from accusations in the world? Can people accuse you accurately of faithfulness to God? No matter what others say or do, we are to give no cause for accusation in a worldly way. Ultimately this frustrates Satan's plans. When we live above reproach, the only thing left for the world to rely upon for an accusation is our expressed love for the Lord.

Has sleep left you? Is your stress level such that you toss and turn all night? Are you one who has difficultly turning off your mind and leaving it with the Lord? Meditate upon Him; recount and remember His past faithfulness in your life. He will give you rest when you know you have done all you could to be faithful before God and man. Therefore, rest your head on your pillow and allow the Lord to work through it all. Make that conscious effort as you retire to leave everything in His loving, capable hands.

In peace I will both lie down and sleep,
For You alone, O LORD, make me to dwell in safety.
—PSALM 4:8

---

[75] Matthew 8:24

My Task/Challenge

_____
_____
_____
_____
_____
_____
_____
_____
_____
_____
_____

My Outcome/Results

_____
_____
_____
_____
_____
_____
_____
_____
_____
_____

DAY 16 ~ *A Flood of Wonders*

I shall remember the deeds of the LORD;
surely I will remember Your wonders of old.
—PSALM 77:11

Sadly, certain "wonders of old" seem to be little more than fairy tales in the eyes of many people today. For example, many view the cataclysmic judgment flood of Noah's day as if what adorns nursery walls depicts what actually happened instead of being just a reminder to a small child that God does indeed keep His promises. While we stress the meaning of the rainbow to small children, for the adult who views the flood as a fairy tale, the truth must be told.

The Scriptures state that because of the relentless corruption of humanity, nothing with breath in its nostrils would survive except a small crew of eight faithful souls.[76] Perhaps, in those first few moments of drizzle, the people mocking Noah, his family, and the stream of animals entering that homemade barge felt little sense of foreboding as water gracefully dripped from the sky.

Contrary to the children's artwork we've all seen, this was not a spring shower for forty days. Noah and the friendly animals were not enjoying a perpetual sunny day in the open air on deck, rainbow in the background, as they blissfully floated together.

As the sky thundered with torrential rain, God's Word states that great chasms split open: "All the fountains of the great deep burst open, and the floodgates of the sky were opened."[77] Great tectonic activity moved as water burst forth to the point of covering the highest mountain crest by twenty-two feet.

The people on the outside of the barge could only tread water for so long before exhaustion and terror overtook them. Through the air vents in the ark, I imagine Noah's family could hear the

---

[76] Genesis 6:10, 18
[77] Genesis 7:11

howls of the people, who not only mocked Noah but also God Himself until finally, the last cry fell silent.

Though the Word states that it rained for forty days and nights, the Scriptures also state, "the water prevailed upon the earth one hundred and fifty days."[78] God's power was on full display. He had total control of the elements, from overrunning the earth with water to guiding the barge to its resting place on the mountains of Ararat—from causing the waters to recede to placing a beautiful bow in the sky.

When we remember God's wondrous deeds accurately, we can learn from them. In the flood account, we see His judgment for the chronic, willful sin of those who rejected Him. We also see His faithful, enduring kindness and care for those who loved and trusted Him. We see His restoration, His provision, His clear warning, and of course, that He certainly does keep His promises.

How far from the truth are those adults who would reduce this account to a children's bedtime story! Today, we find marine fossils high upon the tallest mountains. With more than 250 people groups around the world, some having had no recorded contact with each other, they tell of fascinating accounts in their history of a small group of people in a large vessel, saved from a catastrophic flood. God's Word is true, and His deeds are wondrous. The elements are in subjection to Him, and that fact did not change when He came to walk among us.

On Day 15, I mentioned the account of Jesus upon the stormy sea. Today, I want to look at it a bit more closely. The account opens with the disciples putting out to sea while the Lord took a nap. Suddenly, "a fierce gale of wind descended on the lake, and they began to be swamped and to be in danger."[79] The disciples were terrified as their boat rocked, convinced they would perish. In their utter panic, they came to Yeshua, woke Him up, and expressed their fears. At once, "He got up and rebuked the wind and the surging waves, and they stopped, and it became calm."[80]

---

[78] Genesis 7:24
[79] Luke 8:23
[80] Luke 8:24

Does that sound familiar? Only God can control the elements, and His disciples knew it. Their reaction proved that fact as they proclaimed to each other, "Who then is this, that He commands even the winds and the water, and they obey Him?"[81] He is Jesus, the Messiah of Israel, the Creator of the universe who commands the elements to obey Him. Such a fact we should never water down!

Since some of God's wondrous deeds seem far beyond our imagination, we tend to allow imagination to dictate how we view the account. I must confess that, as a new believer, I grappled with the validity of not only a worldwide flood but also whether any of the accounts were true at all. It was the Noah "story" to me. Yet, there is tremendous evidence to support its validity.

Have you investigated the flood account? Many wonderful resources exist for those who struggle to know the truth regarding this catastrophic event.[82] Even beyond our understanding, it is good to know the evidence so that we can help remove the obstacles before those who struggle for answers.

God has not left us without a witness to this worldwide event. Don't take my word for it! Commit to becoming equipped with answers in this area. It is the perfect way to boost your faith—one that will prompt you to remember the deeds of the Lord and His wonders of old.

And in the fourth watch of the night
He came to them, walking on the sea.
But immediately Jesus spoke to them, saying,
"Take courage, it is I; do not be afraid."
—MATTHEW 14:25, 27

---

[81] Luke 8:25

[82] Visit www.icr.org for great information on this topic.

My Task/Challenge

_____

_____

_____

_____

_____

_____

_____

_____

_____

_____

My Outcome/Results

_____

_____

_____

_____

_____

_____

_____

_____

_____

_____

DAY 17 ~ *A Healthy Fear of the Lord*

But the lovingkindness of the LORD is from
everlasting to everlasting on those who fear Him,
and His righteousness to children's children,
to those who keep His covenant
and remember His precepts to do them.
—PSALM 103:17–18

God's lovingkindness falls upon *those who fear Him*. Those believers who · fear Him are those who keep His covenant. They not only remember His precepts, but they *do* them. They live by those precepts. What prompts their obedience, it seems, is their *fear* of the Lord.

Believers and unbelievers alike can misunderstand the *fear* of the Lord. Some time ago, after I had conducted a talk on the problem of evil and human suffering, one gentleman, in particular, seemed to have great difficulty with what I had shared. With Bible in hand, he approached me. "Now, I'm not trying to be argumentative or anything," he said. "I just want to understand . . ." And then off he went in an attempt to prove to me that God was the author of evil.

We went back and forth for a while as he turned to proof text after proof text. His "proof" was easily refutable since he read the Scriptures out of context. The amazing thing was that, after I showed him the flaw in his use of a verse, he never refuted me—he simply moved on to another verse. His technique was reminiscent of conversations I've had with folks in cults. When they don't like what I'm explaining to them regarding the Word of God, they simply move on to another verse.

After addressing his concern in many different ways, I realized that perhaps his staunch belief that God was the author of evil was not his real objection. There had to be something else at the root of his intense desire to accuse God.

Finally, without breaking eye contact, I said, "I have answered you with Scripture and sound reason in many different ways. Since this is obviously not your real objection, I am asking you point-blank, *what is your question?*"

An old sales axiom states, "He who talks first loses." I was not going to peep until he revealed his actual obstacle to belief. It took a while, but I remained unfazed, unblinking, and quiet. Suddenly, the expression on his face changed. It was as though he was thinking deeply for the first time during our discussion. Finally, he humbly confessed, "I fear God . . . I mean, I, I am terrified of God."

Filled with compassion, I replied, "Okay, imagine you're in high school, and every day you see the principal standing in the hallway as he observes the students pass by. You see him, but your eyes quickly dart away from him. You fear him."

He said, "Yes, he's the guy who holds the paddle."

I then explained, "Right, he's got all the power and authority to make your life good or miserable. Now, imagine that one day as you pass him by, he approaches you and asks if he could join you for lunch. Reluctantly, you agree. As you munch on your sandwiches, he asks you how things are going. He helps you with some math problems and then asks your permission to join you for lunch again the following day.

"After a while, you realize the principal actually does care about you and what is best for you. Though he still holds the paddle, you understand it is necessary to prevent those who would stray in the wrong direction from doing so. Suddenly, you realize you still fear him, but now you do so in a healthy way. It is the same with God. You, my friend, need to learn of Him through the Scriptures. You need to see His loving character and attributes. You need to learn to fear Him in a healthy way." The man slowly nodded in agreement and genuinely thanked me, and that ended our discussion.

Days later, I found out the man was a plant. He was a staunch atheist who held several degrees, one of them in theology, which he had obtained to rock the faith of unequipped believers. He'd heard that I would be speaking at that venue and wanted to have a little chat. Somehow, I don't think our meeting worked out the way he planned.

Joseph of old was another man who feared the Lord. His *healthy* fear of the Lord prevented him from succumbing to the advances of Potiphar's wife. He chose to run out of the house naked rather than to compromise. In his response to Mrs. Potiphar, he said, "How then could I do this great evil and sin against God?"[83]

Joseph knew that ultimately, all sin is against the Lord. He wanted to honor his position and retain Potiphar's trust, but he also knew that physical intimacy with Potiphar's wife would do damage to his spiritual intimacy with God. Joseph's fear was appropriate, and God would later esteem his faithfulness. Though he was falsely accused and jailed, Joseph would eventually hold a place of highest honor.

Then, of course, there are those who look good on the outside, but when push comes to shove, they do not *fear* anyone. Enter Ananias and Sapphira. Many in the early church were selling property and giving money to the assembly. I imagine the praise they received for doing so prompted this couple to do the same. Unfortunately, they conspired to lie about the price they earned so they could pocket the rest. Peter was stunned that they would lie about this since it was their land to begin with, and they could have kept the entire sum of cash if they chose. Peter explained, "You have not lied to men but to God."[84]

If Ananias and Sapphira had realized a healthy fear of the Lord, this behavior might not have ever entered their minds. Their separate lies before the assembly proved they were both in the same spiritual condition, and as a result, they suffered the same demise. They died on the spot. Now that is what I call *church discipline*! The impact was significant, and everyone in the fellowship realized that the Lord was involved in the intimate details of their lives.

A healthy fear of the Lord prompts an obedient life that leads to experiencing the Lord's lovingkindness. An unhealthy fear of the

---

[83] Genesis 39:9
[84] Acts 5:4

Lord causes us to hold Him at arm's length and, therefore, believe we can do our own thing without consequence. Since we do not think anyone will learn of our moments of compromise, it prompts us to deceive not only others but also ourselves.

Do you have a healthy or unhealthy fear of the Lord? What you do when you are alone, and what you communicate or do before others, will answer this question. Take time today to examine your heart in this area. Remember, "The fear of the Lord is the beginning of wisdom."[85]

So the church throughout all Judea and Galilee and Samaria enjoyed peace, being built up; and going on in the fear of the Lord and in the comfort of the Holy Spirit, it continued to increase.
—ACTS 9:31

---

[85] Psalm 111:10, Proverbs 9:10

My Task/Challenge

_____

_____

_____

_____

_____

_____

_____

_____

_____

_____

_____

My Outcome/Results

_____

_____

_____

_____

_____

_____

_____

_____

_____

_____

_____

DAY 18 ~ *Bearing His Image*

Remember His wonders which He has done,
His marvels and the judgments uttered by His mouth.
—PSALM 105:5

When you think of God's wonders and marvels, certainly the creation account must come to mind, and specifically the creation of those He made in His image and likeness. What a heady, astonishing act this was! And how many powerful truths and implications it exposes.

In the passages regarding the creation of humankind, there is a hint to the tri-unity of God. We find the words, "Let *Us* make man in *Our* image, according to *Our* likeness."[86] What does this mean? What does it mean that God created us in His image and likeness? That question alone must prompt wonder in the minds of those who sincerely reflect upon it.

Because an omnipresent God cannot be contained in a body, "likeness" must refer to humankind as made in His spiritual image. Humanity's spirit is immortal, reflective, desiring, willing, powerful, craving unity, and pleasure with and in our Creator. From this, we understand why to murder another image bearer is a great sin. We can recognize that to indulge in depraved passions is to degrade our image. When we backbite, falsely accuse, or curse another human being, this is equivalent to defaming the One in Whose image we bear. Besides, the likeness of God in us is the reason why it is a sin and great folly to elevate creatures above the Creator.[87] The proper order of God's creation is that fish, birds, and beasts are in subjection to Him and then to His image-bearers.[88]

Have you ever noticed that God created humankind last? Did He save the best for last, or did He just want to prove to egotistical humanity that He did not need our help, advice, or ingenuity?

---

[86] Genesis 1:26
[87] Romans 1:25
[88] Genesis 1:26

Perhaps this creation order is because He did not want to set his image-bearers in a waste place but in a lush and beautiful environment, fitted perfectly for their every need. Indeed, the Father, Son, and Holy Spirit took a personal interest in the creative process, since it is to God, revealed through His Triune Being, that we are to devote ourselves with all heart, soul, mind, and strength in a perfect love relationship.[89]

Nevertheless, we know that the first love relationship was tainted as we tumbled into sin from our lofty station. What awful consequences Adam and Eve suffered for their disobedience! Shame, fear, pride, spiritual death, and ultimately physical death were the immediate results of their sin.

The second part of today's verse points to "judgments uttered by His mouth." God first uttered His judgments upon His image-bearers in Genesis 3 (it might be a good idea to refresh yourself if you are unfamiliar with this chapter). The serpent's physiology changed to that of a snake in the grass that would later receive a head-crushing blow. Since the text states that God cursed the serpent *more* than the beasts and cattle of the field, it implies that the effects of the fall fell upon the other creatures as well. To the woman, childbearing would be a painful, difficult experience, and though she desired to be the one with authority over the man, her husband would rule over her.

As for Adam, no longer would he simply cultivate the garden. As a result of his disobedience, he would have to attain his sustenance through hard labor. The creation itself was subject to the fall as, suddenly, new-formed thorns and thistle made his task difficult. Since Adam and Eve had decided to act as God, determining what was good and evil for themselves, God cast them out of the garden. They were never to eat of the *Tree of Life* while in that fallen condition. If they had access to that tree's fruit, all humanity would live forever in their sin condition.

Habitual sin, death, broken fellowship, and a fractured divine image were the tragic results of the fall. However, within those uttered judgments, there was the promise of One whose heel would be bruised while delivering a crushing blow to the head of that *Serpent of Old*.

---

[89] Genesis 1:26, John 1:1–3

When we remember the wonders God has done and the judgments of His mouth, we see our Savior stooped over, writing on the ground with His finger. Men clenching rocks in their fists surround Him, and an immoral and terrified woman angrily tossed to the ground. They are her accusers and potential executioners. What does He write in the dust? Is it the sin with which the men were engaged? Did He write the names of those men who had immoral relationships with her? Was He writing the Decalogue, reminding them of the Law of Moses?

He straightened Himself from His stooped position and invited them, "He who is without sin among you, let him be the first to throw a stone at her." Again, He stooped to write, but it appeared that folks would rather not stay to read what He scrawled. By the time He returned to a standing position, all were gone except Himself and the woman. After a brief dialogue on the puzzling whereabouts of those who originally condemned her, He tenderly told the woman, "I do not condemn you, either. Go. From now on sin no more." Rather than a brutal execution on that day, the woman received Yeshua's forgiveness and His warning to change her ways. Her propensity for sin was a result of the fall; her changed life was the result of His compassion on a lost sinner who sought His forgiveness.

While we bear His spiritual likeness, Jesus, who bore our physical likeness, told Nicodemus:

> "For God did not send the Son into the world to judge the world, but that the world might be saved through Him. He who believes in Him is not judged; he who does not believe has been judged already, because he has not believed in the name of the only begotten Son of God."[90]

Wondrous and marvelous, it is indeed that He came bearing our physical likeness! While bearing our physical likeness, He restored our fractured divine image and our broken relationship with the Triune God. He does not need to condemn us since we condemn ourselves simply by our unbelief. His judgments are true. His wisdom is everlasting.

---

[90] John 3:17–18

Have you considered the fact that God created you in His image? Have you considered how elevating that is? Have you considered your attitude toward your fellow man? Do you entertain yourself with programs that degrade the image of God by having contestants do detestable things for money? I often wonder whose behavior is worse—the one who carries out these detestable acts or those who entertain themselves by them.

Do particular comments, even in jest, expose your true feelings about your fellow image-bearers? That is a hard one that we are all guilty of as we live life in the *culture of mean*. Examine your heart today in this regard. God judges our thoughts. Thus the judgments He utters are just. One of the wonders He has done was to create you in His image, according to His likeness. Therefore, petition Him today to reveal to you what it means to bear His image, and then live accordingly.

"Bring My sons from afar and
My daughters from the ends of the earth,
Everyone who is called by My name,
and whom I have created for My glory,
Whom I have formed, even whom I have made."
—ISAIAH 43:6–7

My Task/Challenge

_____

_____

_____

_____

_____

_____

_____

_____

_____

_____

_____

My Outcome/Results

_____

_____

_____

_____

_____

_____

_____

_____

_____

_____

_____

DAY 19 ~ *The Lord's Lovingkindness*

Who is wise? Let him give heed to these things,
And consider the lovingkindnesses of the LORD.
—PSALM 107:43

hen we read the Scriptures, allowing them to speak for themselves, we would have to be intellectually dishonest to miss the Lord's lovingkindness. As I read my Bible cover to cover for the first time shortly after giving Him my life, His loving-kindnesses were overwhelming. Today's verse states that wise people will pause to consider this fact.

One passage that immediately comes to mind might seem a bit obscure, but for me, it speaks of the heart of God. The first time I read it, it unexpectedly brought me to tears. We find it in, of all places, the book of Exodus:

> "If you ever take your neighbor's cloak as a pledge, you are to return it to him before the sun sets, for that is his only covering; it is his cloak for his body. What else shall he sleep in? And it shall come about that when he cries out to Me, I will hear him, for I am gracious."[91]

In the middle of laws dealing with all kinds of matters, civil and judicial, God commands that if anyone takes a person's cloak as his promise to pay a debt, the person who received it must give it back before sundown. Why? Because he needs it for a covering as he sleeps, he needs it for warmth and will be cold without it. I cannot help but picture a person so desperate in his situation that he would have to offer this invaluable possession, the very thing that would provide warmth, to help him with an even greater need. Yet the Lord will hear that individual as he cries out to Him in his distress if the person who took it does not return it before chilly nightfall.

---

[91] Exodus 22:26–27

Also, I love how the Lord makes a case for returning that cloak. "For that is his only covering; it is his cloak for his body. What else shall he sleep in?" It is as if the Lord is appalled at the thought of someone being so hardhearted that they would not return such an item before sundown. How precious is that?

It is astonishing to realize that the God of all creation, the One with all power, the Almighty God, cares about what would seem to be such a minute thing. Yet it is not a small matter to God, because it is not a trivial matter for that troubled and distressed person who cries out to Him. In the same psalm that includes our opening verse, we repeatedly read, "Then they cried out to the LORD in their trouble; He delivered them out of their distresses."[92]

The cloak was a vital piece of clothing, yet we read of one man who gladly tossed it away for something far better. Jesus, Yeshua the Messiah, as He was leaving Jericho, took time for a man whom everyone else tried to *hush up*. Blind Bartimaeus heard a commotion and at once surmised that Jesus was near. He cried out to the Lord in his distress, though others around him rebuked him for doing so. Nevertheless, the more they told him to hush, the louder his cries to the Lord became.

Jesus would not continue His journey without first displaying His great lovingkindness toward one who called upon Him in faith. By referring to Jesus as the "Son of David,"[93] the blind man was acknowledging his belief that Yeshua was undeniably the Messiah. He believed Jesus to be who He said He was.

The Scripture states that Jesus stopped and told the people to call the blind man to come to Him. "Throwing aside his cloak, he jumped up and came to Jesus."[94] Now that is zeal for the Lord! Recall how vital the cloak was—how badly this man would have needed it. Yet so great was his need to meet Jesus, that he gladly tossed it aside. The text also states that he "jumped up and came to Jesus." This blind beggar expected to be the recipient of his Lord's lovingkindness—and he was. Yeshua asked him what he wanted as if He did not know, and of course, his request was to regain his

---

[92] Psalm 107:6, 13, 19, 28
[93] Mark 10:47
[94] Mark 10:50

sight. Yeshua healed Bartimaeus, and he became an even more passionate and active follower.

Our opening verse asked, "Who is wise?" There is wisdom in recognizing that loving-kindnesses flow from the Lord. The verse reminds us to heed, or consider, His loving-kindnesses of the past. In doing this, we have hope for the future.

Do you feel that your concerns are too small to bring to the Lord? Do you lack the confidence and zeal of Bartimaeus because it is hard for you to accept the fact that God could care about all that concerns you?

No matter how insignificant you think your challenge is, lay it all out before the Lord today. His lovingkindness is always available, and so is His power to express it toward believers who, by faith, trust that they will be recipients.

"Do not worry then, saying, 'What will we eat?' or
'What will we drink?' or 'What will we wear for clothing?'
For the Gentiles eagerly seek all these things;
for your heavenly Father knows that you need all these things.
But seek first His kingdom and His righteousness,
and all these things will be added to you."
—MATTHEW 6:31–33

My Task/Challenge

_____

_____

_____

_____

_____

_____

_____

_____

_____

_____

My Outcome/Results

_____

_____

_____

_____

_____

_____

_____

_____

_____

_____

DAY 20 ~ *Raising Hands To His Commands*

And I shall lift up my hands to Your commandments,
which I love; and I will meditate on Your statutes.
—PSALM 119:48

---

*K*ing David proclaimed that he loved and honored the Lord's commandments to the point of lifting his hands in spontaneous, worshipful meditation upon His statutes.

David knew that meditating upon God's will would produce a life that naturally *lived* God's will. As I read Psalm 119, I cannot help but feel David's passion throughout it. He reveals so much of his heart and love for the Lord and his desire to please Him. David realized that the more he meditated upon the Lord's statutes and commandments, the more natural it would be for him to follow and teach others as well.

David understood something that many folks tend to miss. What our culture arrogantly rejects was evident to him: "For it is not an idle word for you; indeed it is your life. And by this word, you will prolong your days in the land."[95] God's Word, commandments, and statutes are for our good. They help us live life the way we should live in a fallen world.

When David went from shepherd to king, he understood that if he governed according to God's statutes, wise government and peaceful society would naturally flow from his rule. Oh, how important it is for leaders to understand that God's Word is for their, and our, good! How sad that people often accuse God's Word of stealing their fun when the reality is just the opposite. By following His Word, they can experience a fuller, more healthy, joyful, and peaceful life.

Some believe that if they never read God's law, they will remain unaccountable to it. However, they will have a hard time

---

[95] Deuteronomy 32:47

getting away with that excuse. The apostle Paul explained why in the book of Romans.

> For when Gentiles who do not have the Law do instinctively the things of the Law, these, not having the Law, are a law to themselves, in that they show the work of the Law written in their hearts, their conscience bearing witness and their thoughts alternately accusing or else defending them.[96]

Even without reading the Ten Commandments, anyone can know the moral law. We all follow it or break it, and we know when we do this because, as we just read, *it is written upon our hearts*. In other words, it is intuitive.

During a tense time, a lawyer who was testing Jesus had the following conversation with Him:

> "Teacher, which is the great commandment in the Law?"

> [Yeshua] said to [the lawyer], "'YOU SHALL LOVE THE LORD YOUR GOD WITH ALL YOUR HEART, AND WITH ALL YOUR SOUL, AND WITH ALL YOUR MIND.' This is the great and foremost commandment. The second is like it, 'YOU SHALL LOVE YOUR NEIGHBOR AS YOURSELF.' On these two commandments depend the whole Law and the Prophets."[97]

The whole Mosaic Law and the writings of the prophets can be summed up in loving God above all and loving other people as you love yourself. If our society followed these two commandments, which we know intuitively, what a wonderful world it would be indeed!

Paul also wrote, "Owe nothing to anyone except to love one another, for he who loves his neighbor has fulfilled the law."[98] If you want to fulfill the law of God, love one another. By loving God and each other, as Moses said, we will prolong our days.

---

[96] Romans 2:14–15
[97] Matthew 22:36–40
[98] Romans 13:8

Loving our neighbor as ourselves implies we already engage in self-love. Unfortunately, the truth of this is veiled to many because our culture tries desperately to condone various bad behaviors by declaring that our challenge lies in the thinking that we don't love ourselves enough! However, God's Word is true. Why do you think many people become angry or depressed so easily? Much of the time, it is because they believe they deserve better than their present circumstances, and this is the self-love ingratitude problem.

Reread and think about those words from today's opening psalm. Can you honestly state that you *love* God's commandments and statutes? Do you love them so much that you are willing to internalize them, allowing them to change you from the inside out as David did? If you lift your hands in praise to the Lord, can you honestly lift your hands in praise to the moral law that He has written upon your heart?

Seriously consider the questions above. Where you see a weakness in your life, go before the Lord and confess it. If it involves another person, ask his or her forgiveness as well. God will be pleased, and you will be blessed and be a blessing to many others.

"A new commandment I give to you,
that you love one another, even as I have loved you,
that you also love one another.
By this all men will know that you are My disciples,
if you have love for one another."
—JOHN 13:34–35

My Task/Challenge

_____
_____
_____
_____
_____
_____
_____
_____
_____
_____

My Outcome/Results

_____
_____
_____
_____
_____
_____
_____
_____
_____
_____

DAY 21 ~ *The Lord will Revive*

I will never forget Your precepts,
For by them You have revived me.
—PSALM 119:93

I love today's verse because it reminds me of my frailty. It reminds me that each one of us can easily, and without warning, come to a place where we need a little reviving, and God's Word is the perfect place to start.

Elijah was one such man who needed a spiritual and physical revival. If you read the account of him challenging and humiliating the 450 prophets of Baal, you might find it hard to believe he ever reached such a low point. Surely, we cannot help but imagine a man of great strength! What a scene it must have been: the people apathetic, Baal's prophets cutting themselves as they called upon their god to consume their sacrifice with fire, screaming at the top of their lungs past midday and into the evening. Unfortunately for them, not so much as a spark flew from all that hot air to penetrate their sacrifice.

After a long day of enduring 450 prophets' ear-splitting cries as Elijah engaged in a bit of a comedy routine at their expense, he calmly repaired the altar of the Lord. Elijah placed an offering upon it then drenched it three times with water, filling the trench he'd built around it. Once the sacrifice and the altar were saturated, and it was time for the evening sacrifice, he calmly prayed:

> "O LORD, the God of Abraham, Isaac and Israel, today let it be known that You are God in Israel and that I am Your servant and I have done all these things at Your word. Answer me, O LORD, answer me, that this people may know that You, O LORD, are God, and that You have turned their heart back again."[99]

---

[99] 1 Kings 18:36–37

To say that what happened next was dramatic would be an understatement. Fire fell from heaven and consumed the offering, the wood, the stones, the dust, and every drop of water in that trench. What was the response of the people who just witnessed all this? They were apathetic no longer as they broke out in spontaneous, uncontrollable exaltations of, "The LORD, He is God; the LORD, He is God"![100] Elijah then had the prophets of Baal seized and brought down to the brook Kishon, where he slew every one of them.

After this dramatic event, Elijah outran King Ahab's chariot from Carmel to Jezreel, where he heard the news that Jezebel, Ahab's wicked wife, was determined to take his life by the next evening. Fear gripped him as he ran for his life to Beersheba. He went a day's journey into the wilderness, sat under a juniper tree, requested to die, and then finally laid down and slept.

What happened? Why would Elijah be so bold before Ahab, the people, and 450 prophets of Baal and yet be terrified of a woman named Jezebel? I think the answer is obvious. Elijah was exhausted—he was physically, spiritually, and emotionally drained. As a frail human being, there was nothing left within him. The good news is that the Lord understood that Elijah needed to be revived not only with food and drink but also with His Word.

An angel encouraged Elijah to arise and eat, providing food for him. Then, we read that "the angel of the LORD" came to him a second time saying, "Arise, eat, because the journey is too great for you."[101] Yes, the Lord knows what we need, and when we need it! He knows what we need to sustain us for our journey before, during, and after. That meal sustained Elijah for forty days. When we see him again, he's having a bit of a pity party in a cave at Horeb, where the Lord Himself encouraged him. *Jehovah-Jireh*, The Lord Will Provide, is also the Lord Who will revive.

Elijah was a strong man in the Lord, but came to the end of himself in strength and required outside refreshing and provision. In like manner, Yeshua, Jesus our Lord, was a strong man who endured much even before He came to the garden of Gethsemane. Yet once there, fully God and fully man, He anguished in His

---

[100] 1 kings 18:39
[101] 1 kings 19:7

humanity over what He would soon face: betrayal, arrest, a mock trial, beating, scourging, crucifixion, and the weight of the sin of the world upon Himself. As we read earlier, His sweat was as drops of blood. Nevertheless, He sought to fulfill the Father's will—His precepts, which He loved. As the disciples, who He instructed to watch and pray, were sleeping on the job, the Scriptures state, "Now an angel from heaven appeared to Him, strengthening Him."[102] The Father provided what His Son needed to revive Him in that emotionally and spiritually torturous hour.

God does not remove us from the task He requires of us. He did not remove the cup of suffering from Jesus. Even though He will allow us to come to the end of ourselves, He will provide what we need to move forward to accomplish the task.

Are you exhausted? Do you need to be revived? Do you allow yourself to become exhausted to the point of despair? All too often, we seek revival among the wrong things. We commiserate with friends who tell us what we want to hear: *Why don't you just quit? Look at what this is doing to you. Give up now while you can.*

We reach for unhealthy foods in an attempt to comfort our despair. Or, we release repressed anger and smash anything in sight. Those outbursts cost us much more than just the replacement of broken things!

Yet in God's Word, His precepts, we learn that we can do all things through Him who strengthens us.[103] We learn that He will never leave us or forsake us. We learn the right path and the honorable way to go. We learn by His precepts how to avoid deception and defeat when we feel beaten down and at the end of our fraying rope.

Yeshua is always there. He knows how it feels to be in emotional agony and physical exhaustion. He knows the impact of ministering angels to a hurting soul and the refreshing voice of His Word in our lives. He provides it all, even when we feel too weak to pray. Does that surprise you? He knows when we are at a point where even prayer becomes a task too heavy for us.

---

[102] Luke 22:43
[103] Philippians 4:13

Are you at that point today? He knows all about it. Not a tear falls without His notice. Lean hard upon Him, and if you love His Word, there is no doubt that He will revive you through it.

Consider how I love Your precepts;
Revive me, O LORD, according to Your lovingkindness.
—PSALM 119:159

My Task/Challenge

_____

_____

_____

_____

_____

_____

_____

_____

_____

_____

_____

My Outcome/Results

_____

_____

_____

_____

_____

_____

_____

_____

_____

_____

DAY 22 ~ *Feeling Small and Despised*

I am small and despised, yet I do not forget Your precepts.
—PSALM 119:141

When I think of someone small and despised, young David comes to mind—facing that ten-foot giant, Goliath of Gath. Goliath was not the only one who despised David's actions. His brothers were not too thrilled about him either.

The events began when David was obedient to his father's request, bringing food to his brothers on the front lines as they faced the Philistines. He was to bring back word to their father, Jesse, of their welfare.

As David stood near the battle line chatting with his brothers, Goliath appeared, challenging Israel to send someone out to fight him. Upon hearing the giant's remarks, David asked:

"What will be done for the man who kills this Philistine and takes away the reproach from Israel? For who is this uncircumcised Philistine, that he should taunt the armies of the living God?"[104]

David was overwhelmingly provoked by Goliaths challenge! However, his brothers were not impressed. I imagine they felt he would make them look bad. After all, they were the ones daily facing the battle. Yet they did seem conveniently deaf to the giant's dare.

David's oldest brother, Eliab, burned in anger toward David as he scolded, "Why have you come down? And with whom have you left those few sheep in the wilderness?"[105]

Eliab's goal was to humiliate and belittle David's work as a shepherd. He referred to David as not just a lowly shepherd, but that only a "few sheep" were in his charge. What an insult! Eliab's

---

[104] 1 Samuel 17:26
[105] 1 Samuel 17:28–29

rebuking of David did not end there. He went on to imagine he could read David's heart and intentions: "I know your insolence and the wickedness of your heart; for you have come down in order to see the battle."

David's reaction said it all. "What have I done now? Was it not just a question?" His response proves this was not the first time David felt dismissed, misjudged, accused of mischief, and treated like a fool by his sibling. However, nothing could be further from the truth than Eliab's accusation. Had David's heart not been pure, he would never have had a victory over the giant. He clung to God's precepts and knew the Lord would be with him. David did not need a rebuke from his older sibling; his sibling should have commended him for his righteous indignation toward the challenge against God's people.

Young people who are viewed as foolish, lesser, despised, and rebuked were nothing new to our Lord. In Mark's gospel, we read of people bringing children to Yeshua so that He might touch them. Whether these were parents, guardians, or teachers, the Scriptures do not say, but it does state that the disciples rebuked them for doing this. After all, why bother the Master with small, insignificant, foolish little kids?

When Jesus saw the disciples rebuking folks for bringing the children to Him, the Word states that He was "indignant."

"Permit the children to come to Me; do not hinder them; for the kingdom of God belongs to such as these. Truly I say to you, whoever does not receive the kingdom of God like a child will not enter it at all." And He took them in His arms and began blessing them, laying His hands on them.[106]

When I visit Christian bookstores, artwork depicting Yeshua's love for young children reminds me of this incident. His example in the above passage is one He commands us to follow. After all, in Matthew's Gospel, we read that the disciples came to Jesus with the same question many people still have today: "Who then is greatest in the kingdom of heaven?" To their shock, Yeshua called a child to Him and set the lad before them, saying:

[106] Mark 10:14–16

99

"Truly I say to you, unless you are converted and become like children, you will not enter the kingdom of heaven. Whoever then humbles himself as this child, he is the greatest in the kingdom of heaven. And whoever receives one such child in My name receives Me."[107]

Then came a stern warning from Jesus:

"But, whoever causes one of these little ones who believe in Me to stumble, it would be better for him to have a heavy millstone hung around his neck, and to be drowned in the depth of the sea."[108]

In other words, that person who despises one of His own to the point of leading that little one away from the Messiah would be better off dead. That is quite a warning, wouldn't you say?

Have you ever felt small and despised? I imagine the nation of Israel today feels that way all the time, as they have plenty of enemies surrounding them! Yet we all can sometimes relate; even though no physical battle is against us, we sure are in a spiritual one. However, take heart! The apostle Paul reminds us that:

The foolishness of God is wiser than men, and the weakness of God is stronger than men. For consider your calling, brethren, that there were not many wise according to the flesh, not many mighty, not many noble; but God has chosen the foolish things of the world to shame the wise, and God has chosen the weak things of the world to shame the things which are strong, and the base things of the world and the despised God has chosen, the things that are not, so that He may nullify the things that are, so that no man may boast before God.[109]

Have you convinced yourself that "small and despised" is an apt description for you? If you are in that circumstance today, remember that this surely is not how God sees you. You need a change in perspective. You need, this day, to stop allowing the enemy of your soul to convince you to view yourself in this way and to move forward and serve God as you ought to. He loves the

---

[107] Matthew 18:3–5
[108] Matthew 18:6
[109] 1 Corinthians 1:25–29

children, and you are His child too. He loves you, and He is with you. Therefore, move forward in power to slay those giants in your life and be comforted in His loving arms.

He was despised and forsaken of men,
A man of sorrows and acquainted with grief;
And like one from whom men hide their face
He was despised, and we did not esteem Him.
—ISAIAH 53:3

My Task/Challenge

_____
_____
_____
_____
_____
_____
_____
_____
_____
_____

My Outcome/Results

_____
_____
_____
_____
_____
_____
_____
_____
_____
_____

DAY 23 ~ *Early to Rise*

*I rise before dawn and cry for help; I wait for Your words.
My eyes anticipate the night watches,
that I may meditate on Your word.*
—PSALM 119:147–148

There is something to be said for those early morning hours. That time before the sun has its opportunity to shed its light upon the treetops. It is peaceful. Even the birds are quiet in their nests.

Yet there is power to gain, lessons to learn, and a Presence to experience just before sunrise.

When I read today's verse, I can feel the desperation in the author's tone, and yet there is a confidence that the need will be satisfied because it was brought to the only Person who can answer that cry. Hannah and her husband, Elkanah, experienced that. "They arose early in the morning and worshiped before the Lord."[110] The result of their diligent worship and faithfulness was the birth of little Samuel.

In Judges 6:38, Gideon "arose early the next morning and squeezed the fleece" to see if God had responded to his test. Gideon was up for his Lord's answer at the time of the forming dew. That only happens in the early morning hours.

Another great example of the early-morning seeker is the Proverbs 31 woman. The proverb states that she "rises also while it is still night."[111] This amazing woman understood the value of so many things. But she felt it was especially important to be an early riser to prepare her heart, soul, and mind for her many duties throughout her day.

Getting up early to seek God is not a matter of trying to feel holy or better than other believers do. It's not an opportunity to

[110] 1 Samuel 1:19
[111] Proverbs 31:15

brag about how early you get up and what a great sacrifice you made for the Lord. It is truly anticipating the reality of God's voice. It is the confidence that He has an answer for what concerns you in His Word if you will only seek it and listen for His voice alone before all the distractions of this life set in.

Is it worth it to be there when God speaks? Is it worth it to get away alone to pursue what He might have to speak to you? Is it worth it to cry out to Him in the early morning hours, to know He hears your desperate plea and has the power to do something about that need or to give clear direction? Jesus thought so. We read in the book of Mark that:

> In the early morning, while it was still dark, Jesus got up, left the house, and went away to a secluded place, and was praying there.[112]

What a wonderful example! These precious hours as the day begins are so important. Notice that Yeshua went to a secluded place. He went away from life's distractions. Oh, how important that is!

In this techno age, many individuals tie themselves so tightly to their technology that seclusion from it seems all but impossible. Sometimes I think the use—or overuse—of these things become tools of the enemy of our soul, who would hate us to experience any stillness or quietness as we anticipate the Lord's gentle whisper in our ear. Sometimes I think technology keeps many of us up so late that arising early in the morning is nearly impossible. There are just too many video games to play, too many *apps* to discover, or too many shows on the television or tablet that draws our attention away. We hear voices from everywhere around the world, yet neglect the One most important.

God's Word admonishes us regarding the desire to sleep until the very last moment, just to the point where the start of our day becomes a mad dash: "How long will you lie down, O sluggard? When will you arise from your sleep?"[113]

Now, just because you are not necessarily a morning person does not mean you are a sluggard. However, ask yourself the

---

[112] Mark 1:35
[113] Proverbs 6:9

question, *Do I sincerely have a desire to seek His will, even if it needs to happen first thing in the morning?* My book *The Emmaus Conversation* was born out of an early-morning inspiration after reading Luke 24. I received *orders from headquarters* to create—based upon Scripture, fulfilled prophecy, tradition, archeology, and historical evidence—the compelling discussion between *The Stranger*, who was actually the resurrected Lord, and the two disciples on the road to Emmaus. The orders to write that book came to me during an early morning time of devotion.

What are your thoughts regarding the dedication of the firstfruits of your day to the Lord? If you do not already have an early morning devotional time, what impact do you think it would make on your life if you started meeting God at sunrise? Are you willing to find out? This evening, turn off the television, video game, smartphone, whatever it is that keeps you up late so that you can go to sleep early and rise early.

Anticipate your meeting with the Lord. He states in His Word, "I love those who love me; and those who diligently seek me will find me."[114] Meet Him early, anticipate His presence, and watch the power flow through your day. Trust me. Eventually, you will look forward to your daybreak meetings quietly alone with Him.

In the morning, O LORD, You will hear my voice;
In the morning I will order my prayer to You and eagerly watch.
—PSALM 5:3

---

[114] Proverbs 8:17

My Task/Challenge

_____

_____

_____

_____

_____

_____

_____

_____

_____

_____

My Outcome/Results

_____

_____

_____

_____

_____

_____

_____

_____

_____

DAY 24 ~ *The Power of Remembrance*

I remember the days of old; I meditate on all Your doings;
I muse on the work of Your hands.
I stretch out my hands to You;
my soul longs for You, as a parched land.
—PSALM 143:5–6

*H*ave you ever felt like the psalmist in the above passage? Has your soul ever felt the desperation of being in a spiritually parched land? As we reach the middle point of this devotional, I want to emphasize the importance of recounting, or reviewing, or remembering as the cure for a parched soul.

The treatment for spiritual thirst is a meditation on all the Lord has done throughout history. A review from His marvelous acts of creation to His sacrifice for our sin, which prompts us to look forward to the fulfillment of Revelation 1:7: "Behold, He is coming with the clouds, and every eye will see Him."

I think by now you can see how much the Old Covenant saints understood the importance of recounting, or proclaiming repeatedly, God's marvelous works. In Exodus 15, Moses burst forth with a song praising God, proclaiming the demise of Pharaoh's army, which he had just witnessed. We find the same attitude in Nehemiah 9, with a prayer recounting Israel's history. By retelling the Lord's works as a prayer, it is as if the people were reminding God and themselves that, since He came through in the past, He certainly would and could come through in the future.

Sometimes historical review was for praise, sometimes it was to remind God of His past faithfulness, and sometimes it was merely a reminder to the people of warning or blessing. In Joshua 24, for example, Joshua spoke on behalf of God Himself as he reminded the people of their history. The principle was to remember His commands, love, works, or faithfulness, whether the people were faithful at the time or not.[115]

In Deuteronomy 6, all of Israel was commanded to recount to their children the will of God and His supernatural working in their lives.[116] They were never to forget; therefore, oral transmission was imperative.

In the New Covenant Scriptures, we find more instances of individuals recounting events and times of God's awesome power and goodness. Peter's great sermon in Acts 2 included a retelling of biblical prophecies infused with the identity of Yeshua. As a result, three thousand souls were transformed on Pentecost into new creations for the kingdom.

Stephen began his defense before the Sanhedrin in Acts 7 by recounting the history of Israel and God's remarkable deliverance. One Sabbath day, the apostle Paul in a synagogue at Pisidian Antioch, offered a retelling not only of Israel's history and God's impact in it but also of Jesus the Messiah. He recounted the events of Yeshua's life from His baptism to His death, burial, resurrection, and post-resurrection appearances.

Also, there were times when the purpose of reviewing the past was to offer clarity for those who were confused or who doubted. That is what took place when the resurrected Lord recounted and revealed Himself in the Scriptures, "beginning with Moses and all the prophets," on the road to Emmaus with Cleopas and an unnamed disciple.[117] Yeshua offered a powerful apologetic of Himself to those two dismayed and downcast souls, revealing who He was and is throughout all of history and His Word.

As we consider how important it is to remember the days of old and to meditate on the entirety of Lord's doings, we have to ask ourselves a question. What impact can a recounting of former things have on *our* lives? When we search the Scriptures, we find God's character. We find that He has compassion and is mighty to save. We find that He has kept His people miraculously against all

---

[115] Joshua 24:1–13
[116] Deuteronomy 6:20–23
[117] Luke 24:27

the odds. When we see that He can and does use the most unlikely people, we also understand that there is hope for us.

Surely, you have seen God's rescue at times in your life. He redeems even the most painful circumstances as they became an essential part of our living testimony. Today, stop and think. Take a break from your hurried life and list those times when you knew what you needed was impossible, and you believed there was no way of escape. Take time to note when you, like the children of Israel, had your back against the sea as you watched your enemy in hot pursuit. Note the things God has done in your life and remember to give Him the glory and tell someone else. Who knows, your recounting of God's faithfulness just might lift them out of their parched land!

*"Whoever drinks of the water that I will give him shall never thirst;
but the water that I will give him will become in him
a well of water springing up to eternal life."*
—JOHN 4:14

My Task/Challenge

_____
_____
_____
_____
_____
_____
_____
_____
_____
_____

My Outcome/Results

_____
_____
_____
_____
_____
_____
_____
_____
_____
_____
_____

DAY 25 ~ *Abiding Fruit Bearers*

Consider the work of God,
for who is able to straighten what He has bent?
—ECCLESIASTES 7:13

The verse above is a rhetorical question: God would not be God if anyone could straighten what He has bent! Through our misguided arrogance, we would appreciate the opportunity to reverse the power of God if we felt it was to our advantage. Many times, we think that His way is not fair, and we would intervene if we could. The disobedient traveler, temporary fish treat, and pouting prophet, Jonah, felt that way. He situated himself east of the city of Nineveh, where he had just warned the people of impending judgment, and waited for them to suffer the same fate as Sodom and Gomorrah.

The Lord looked down upon stubborn Jonah, knowing his heart of hatred for those lost people He had commanded him to warn of His impending judgment upon them. The Lord's desire was repentance; Jonah's was revenge.

After urging the people to repent, not thinking they really would, Jonah attempted to build a shelter for himself from the heat of the day as he waited to see the Ninevites get what he felt they deserved. However, God knew that what the prophet constructed was inadequate to protect him from the hot sun. Therefore, God sent a plant to shield him properly.

As Jonah sat comfortably beneath that plant, waiting and hoping all *Gehenna* would break loose upon the wicked people of Nineveh, God, who is the perfect parent, sent a worm to destroy the plant He created. Predictably, stiff-necked Jonah whined, complained, and mourned the loss of that plant to the point of wanting to die along with it. The very plant that God had straightened to shelter Jonah He then bent or destroyed, to teach Jonah a lesson by revealing to him the coldness of his own heart.

111

When the sun came up God appointed a scorching east wind, and the sun beat down on Jonah's head so that he became faint and begged with all his soul to die, saying, "Death is better to me than life."

Then God said to Jonah, "Do you have good reason to be angry about the plant?"

And he said, "I have good reason to be angry, even to death."

Then the LORD said, "You had compassion on the plant for which you did not work and which you did not cause to grow, which came up overnight and perished overnight. Should I not have compassion on Nineveh, the great city in which there are more than 120,000 persons who do not know the difference between their right and left hand, as well as many animals?"[118]

Jonah had compassion for what made him cozy and comfortable yet had no regard for a repentant people—120,000 of them—whom the Lord loved. What God had straightened, He bent to teach Jonah and all who would read the biblical account, that He is powerful, merciful, and responsive to the truly repentant soul on a mass scale.

God is gracious to provide vivid illustrations for His children so that they will never forget His character or the flaws in their own. Thankfully, our Lord does not reveal our flaws to condemn us but to grow and change us into compassionate, productive children for His kingdom.

There was another plant, a fig tree, once as straight as a fig tree can be and full of leaves, yet fruitless. A hungry Jesus "bent" or cursed it as He proclaimed that it would never again bear fruit. The next day, the disciples looked upon what Jesus had cursed. According to Mark's account, seeing the fig tree withered from the roots up, Peter commented, "Rabbi, look, the fig tree which You cursed has withered."[119] From that point on, that tree would be useful only for kindling a fire.

---

[118] Jonah 4:8–11
[119] Mark 11:21

Jesus replied, "Have faith in God,"[120] and then He went on to explain the importance of true belief in prayer. The bending of the fig tree brought about lessons for all who would receive them. The first lesson was that we must be fruitful in the presence of the Lord. The fig tree looked good from a distance, but upon closer inspection, it proved figless. The second lesson has to do with faith in God, and the third lesson is the power of prayer. The power is not in words but in what flows from God, Who hears the believing, pure heart, and answers, resulting in fruitfulness and joy.

These principles are evident in Yeshua's admonishment to his disciples:

"Abide in Me, and I in you. As the branch cannot bear fruit of itself unless it abides in the vine, so neither can you unless you abide in Me. I am the vine, you are the branches; he who abides in Me and I in him, he bears much fruit, for apart from Me you can do nothing. If anyone does not abide in Me, he is thrown away as a branch and dries up; and they gather them, and cast them into the fire and they are burned.

"If you abide in Me, and My words abide in you, ask whatever you wish, and it will be done for you. My Father is glorified by this, that you bear much fruit, and so prove to be My disciples. Just as the Father has loved Me, I have also loved you; abide in My love.

"If you keep My commandments, you will abide in My love; just as I have kept My Father's commandments and abide in His love. These things I have spoken to you so that My joy may be in you, and that your joy may be made full."[121]

The outcome of a pure heart, a faithful prayer, and following what God commands is pure joy. He desires that we live according to His will, which produces joy.

Today, consider these things—your heart and the motives in your prayer life. Consider your attitude toward those you might imagine are so wicked they are beyond our Lord's reach. Perhaps

---

[120] Mark 11:22
[121] John 15:4–11

you are like Jonah, waiting for the fire and brimstone instead of praying for their repentance. Remember that this life is the best it will ever get for those who reject God, and that is pathetically sad. Believe in prayer, that God can move even the mountain of your sour attitude toward specific individuals. He is just that big.

"The seed in the good soil, these are the ones who have heard the word in an honest and good heart, and hold it fast, and bear fruit with perseverance."
—LUKE 8:15

My Task/Challenge

_____

_____

_____

_____

_____

_____

_____

_____

_____

_____

_____

My Outcome/Results

_____

_____

_____

_____

_____

_____

_____

_____

_____

_____

_____

DAY 26 ~ *Rejoice Despite Darkness*

*Indeed, if a man should live many years, let him rejoice in them all,
and let him remember the days of darkness,
for they will be many.*
—ECCLESIASTES 11:8

Today's passage seems like quite a contradiction. We are to rejoice in all our days, yet as we rejoice in them, we are also to remember the dark days, the difficult days, the days we would rather forget.

Solomon, toward the end of his life, jolts us back to reality by forcing us to realize that for many of us, the dark days just might outnumber the good. Yet we are to rejoice even in them.

As we consider this, one cannot help but think of Job and what he suffered, especially the irreplaceable loss of his children. He certainly had many days of darkness. However, someone else comes to my mind when I read the above passage—a man who certainly had many dark days. As a matter of fact, he had more days than anyone ever had before or after him. I am referring to Methuselah.

Methuselah's father was Enoch, who was so close to the Lord's heart that he did not die as we all do. The Scriptures say that "Enoch walked with God; and he was not, for God took him."[122] Poor Methuselah was only three-hundred years old when he lost his dad. I state that lightheartedly. However, can you imagine having such a godly father, who helped you stand firm in the Lord, suddenly vanish after so long a time and without warning? Though he knew his dad was with God, the painful reality was that solid rock, a mighty influence, and godly example for three-hundred years was gone. So what kind of a world did Enoch leave to Methuselah?

---

[122] Genesis 5:24

116

Methuselah was old enough to see his great-grandchildren born to Noah: their familiar names were Ham, Shem, and Japheth. They were over one-hundred years old and Noah six-hundred when Methuselah died. Immediately after his death, the flood prevailed upon the earth.

Methuselah lived during the time Noah was building his barge, a time when "the LORD saw that the wickedness of man was great on the earth and that every intent of the thoughts of his heart was only evil continually."[123]

Can you imagine what it must have been like for Methuselah to witness the godly walk of his father and then to live among the darkest nights of human evil, to the point where God was grieved at having even created humankind?[124] He witnessed so many days of darkness, yet in the midst of that, he could rejoice in the fact that it would be his own grandson's strong stand for the God that would lead to the continuation of humankind on earth.

Fast-forward many centuries later, and we see more dark days during the far shorter life of a man "full of sorrows and acquainted with grief."[125] Yet all of humanity can rejoice in every one of Yeshua's days on this earth.

During our Lord Yeshua's life of just thirty-three years, He knew suffering as no other person ever would. His people rejected Him, and His siblings mocked Him, His fellow citizens accused Him of being insane and of having a demon. The religious leaders renounced Him, and all abandoned Him, including those who claimed they would never leave Him.

Jesus, our Lord, was tempted with every appeal to human flesh yet did not succumb to it. He knew poverty, hunger, thirst, and homelessness. An intimate friend betrayed Him. He was arrested, became the subject of a mock trial, unjustly accused and physically tortured being "marred more than any man and more than the sons of men,"[126] and then sentenced to death though He was completely innocent.

---

[123] Genesis 6:5
[124] Genesis 6:6–8
[125] Isaiah 53:3
[126] Isaiah 52:14

Yet in all the above, every day Jesus walked this earth was a day for rejoicing. During those dark days, the Light of the World walked among us. He cured the sick, the disabled, and the blind. He cast out demons and shamed the devil to his face. He displayed power over the elements and fed thousands with barely enough to feed a family. He prophesied of His crucifixion and resurrection, declared forgiveness of sins, and fulfilled His prophecies by conquering the powers of sin and death.

Yeshua taught humanity how to pray, how to forgive individuals who hurt us, how to come to know God intimately through His Word, and how to live daily in a dark world during very dark days. And the greatest lesson He taught was that because He lives, having risen from the dead, those who put their trust and faith in Him, though they may physically die, their soul will live for all eternity with Him in Heaven.

Because of our Lord's powerful resurrection, we can rejoice in every one of our days as well. We have a living Savior who knows exactly how we feel. He has been there, and He overcame the world just as He said.[127] We can rejoice not only because Jesus understands our pain, but also because He is working out every one of our dark days for our good.[128]

Are you in the midst of dark days? As you live in this fallen world, knowing what is to come, every day might seem dark by comparison. Yet if you are not in a rejoicing mood, perhaps you have lost perspective regarding what awaits you in Heaven.

Do the circumstances of this life constantly steal your ability to rejoice in the bigger picture? Take time today to bring whatever it is that weighs you down and place it at His feet. He uses our life circumstances for His glory when we allow Him to. Trust that since He overcame every obstacle in His life, He can surely overcome yours. Leave it with Him and rejoice.

And it will be said in that day,

---

[127] John 16:33
[128] Romans 8:28

"Behold, this is our God for whom we have waited that He might save us. This is the LORD for whom we have waited;
Let us rejoice and be glad in His salvation."
—ISAIAH 25:9

My Task/Challenge

_____
_____
_____
_____
_____
_____
_____
_____
_____
_____
_____

My Outcome/Results

_____
_____
_____
_____
_____
_____
_____
_____
_____
_____
_____

DAY 27 ~ *A Youthful Perspective*

Remember also your Creator in the days of your youth.
—ECCLESIASTES 12:1

*W*hat great advice to pass on to our children is the passage that opens today's devotional! What excellent counsel for a young person who is trying to live life in a way that pleases the Lord! After all, since the Lord is our Creator, it only makes sense to go to Him for answers. Doing so will make the most significant long-term impact on those who are just starting in life.

Josiah, who I mentioned on Day 9, was one such young man who desired to know God's purpose. Though we read that "Josiah was eight years old when he became king,"[129] he was twenty-seven when he heard the Book of the Law of Moses and immediately responded. Josiah made a public pronouncement regarding where he stood in his relationship to his God:

> The king went up to the house of the LORD and all the men of Judah and all the inhabitants of Jerusalem with him, and the priests and the prophets and all the people, both small and great; and he read in their hearing all the words of the book of the covenant which was found in the house of the LORD.

> The king stood by the pillar and made a covenant before the LORD, to walk after the LORD, and to keep His commandments and His testimonies and His statutes with all his heart and all his soul, to carry out the words of this covenant that were written in this book. And all the people entered into the covenant.[130]

Josiah took care to clean up Jerusalem and rid it of its idolatry. He not only *said* he would follow the Lord, but his

---

[129] 2 kings 22:1–2
[130] 2 kings 23:2–3

actions after that evidenced what had happened to him internally as a young man who remembered his Creator.

Many years later, another youngster was a little older than Josiah was when Josiah became king. This young man made it clear to all who heard Him that He was not about to deviate from His destined path. The King of Kings was only twelve-years-old when, rather than boarding the caravan to head home after celebrating the Passover Feast, He decided to have a chat with the religious leaders of His day.

> After three days [Mary and Joseph] found Him in the temple, sitting in the midst of the teachers, both listening to them and asking them questions. And all who heard Him were amazed at His understanding and His answers.[131]

Jesus not only asked questions that stumped the religious experts of His day, but He also had all the answers to those questions. Once they found Him, Mary and Joseph baffled Jesus by their anxious attitudes and the fact that they needed to search for Him, let alone a search that took three days! Puzzled at their worry, He posed a question: "Why is it that you were looking for Me? Did you not know that I had to be in My Father's house?"[132] Where else would He be?

Children as young as twelve or even eight can have a passion for the right things of the Lord. They can remember their Creator throughout their youth and can be mindful of His will and His ways. Oh, the lessons we can learn from a young heart tender toward his or her Creator! What a great reminder this is for us to bring our children back to that place when they first became curious. Oh, that we would equip ourselves to seize those times and answer their questions.

Perhaps you are in your twenties or thirties. Maybe you are older. Perhaps you've had moments when you have forgotten or forsaken your Creator. What was the outcome? It is not pretty, is it?

---

[131] Luke 2:46–47
[132] Luke 2:49

Take time today to ponder what it means to *remember* the One who created you. Ponder what it means to have a loving Creator; think about the unlimited potential we have in Him. Trust Him, like Josiah. Read His Word and react in a way consistent with what you say you believe. Ask the difficult questions, like Jesus did when He was twelve, and then turn to Him for the answers.

The Everlasting God, the LORD, the Creator of the ends of the earth does not become weary or tired. His understanding is inscrutable. He gives strength to the weary, and to him who lacks might He increases power. Though youths grow weary and tired, and vigorous young men stumble badly, yet those who wait for the LORD will gain new strength; they will mount up with wings like eagles, they will run and not get tired, they will walk and not become weary.
—ISAIAH 40:28–31

My Task/Challenge

_____
_____
_____
_____
_____
_____
_____
_____
_____
_____

My Outcome/Results

_____
_____
_____
_____
_____
_____
_____
_____
_____
_____

DAY 28 ~ *The Eternal "I AM"*

"Give thanks to the LORD, call on His name.
Make known His deeds among the peoples;
make them remember that His name is exalted."
—ISAIAH 12:4

W e have all heard it asked, "What's in a name?" When the name is that of God, there's quite a lot! For Moses, the name of God was a definition he could communicate to Israel that would speak volumes regarding why they could so fully trust in Him.

At the time he learned God's memorial name, Moses was living the low-key life of a shepherd for his father-in-law's flock. His experience as a shepherd was quite a change from Pharaoh's luxurious palace, where he grew up as the son of Pharaoh's daughter. However, working in an obscure place as a lowly shepherd did not disqualify him in the Lord's eyes. God can call us from any station, age, or location, including a solitary burning bush on Horeb, the mountain of God.

From that lonely place, the Lord told Moses to go back to Egypt, despite his self-doubts and fears, where God would use him mightily to deliver his people from bondage. It was there, on Horeb, where Moses asked the Supreme Being for His name:

> Then Moses said to God, "Behold, I am going to the sons of Israel, and I will say to them, 'The God of your fathers has sent me to you.' Now they may say to me, 'What is His name?' What shall I say to them?"

> God said to Moses, "I AM WHO I AM"; and He said, "Thus you shall say to the sons of Israel, 'I AM has sent me to you.'" God, furthermore, said to Moses, "Thus you shall say to the sons of Israel, 'The Lord, the God of your fathers, the God of Abraham, the God of Isaac, and the God of Jacob, has sent me to you.' This

is My name forever, and this is My memorial-name to all generations."[133]

What a name! Simply, I AM. Yet it is not so simple. The great news is that God is not "I Am *For Now*," or "I *Was*," or "Someday I *Hope* To Be," or "I Am *Only* for Moses." God is the eternal *now*, the *I AM*. He did not have a beginning. He will have no end. He does not change. He does not exist simply for one group or one person. He is the I AM; He always was, always has been, and always will be.

What great trust and confidence Moses was able to communicate to Israel concerning the One who called him to lead them, not into a wilderness, but to freedom and a love relationship with God that would set them apart from every pagan culture around them. Also, this God would not be the God of Israel only, but of all who would call upon His name in faith and love.

This awesome God did indeed save a nation from the clutches of an evil pharaoh, but that was in many ways only a foretaste of His grander plan: He is also a God who desires the salvation of the whole world through His only begotten Son.

Isaiah 9:6 is a passage of Scripture that we read and hear every year upon celebrating the incarnation:

> For a child will be born to us, a son will be given to us; and the government will rest on His shoulders; and His name will be called Wonderful Counselor, Mighty God, Eternal Father, Prince of Peace.

We read afterword that "the zeal of the Lord of hosts will accomplish this."[134] He certainly did accomplish it, through a young virgin named Mary:

> "And behold, you will conceive in your womb and bear a son, and you shall name Him Jesus. He will be great and will be called the Son of the Most High; and the Lord God will give Him the throne of His father

---

[133] Exodus 3:13–15
[134] Isaiah 9:6

David; and He will reign over the house of Jacob forever, and His kingdom will have no end."[135]

To a frightened Joseph, Mary's betrothed, who considered breaking that betrothal because of this alarming conception, an angel of the Lord, communicated:

> "Joseph, son of David, do not be afraid to take Mary as your wife; for the Child who has been conceived in her is of the Holy Spirit. She will bear a Son; and you shall call His name Jesus, for He will save His people from their sins."[136]

The Scriptures go on to state:

> Now all this took place to fulfill what was spoken by the Lord through the prophet: "Behold, the virgin shall be with child and shall bear a son, and they shall call his name Immanuel," which translated means, "God with us."[137]

That Child was Jesus the Messiah, the One who does not change, the One who can never leave you or forsake you because He is the I AM. As Jesus said of Himself to those individuals who questioned Him, "Truly, truly, I say to you, before Abraham was born, I AM."[138] The reaction of the people who heard Him use this reference for Himself proves they understood what He was saying. They wanted to stone Him for making Himself out to be God. Before Abraham or anyone else was born, Jesus is the I AM. He is God.

Have you called upon Immanuel lately with the clarity and realization that He is God Himself—that He is the One with the power to save and miraculously influence your life? Have you called upon Him, understanding that since He does not change, His plan and purpose for you does not change either? Have you called upon Him lately, not with your grocery list of wants and desires, but with a sincere desire to know and do His will for your life? I urge you to do that today. He alone can bring clarity for your

---

[135] Luke 1:31–33
[136] Matthew 1:20–21
[137] Matthew 1:22–23
[138] John 8:58 AMP

decisions and point you in the right direction. Trust the I AM—today and every day.

For there is no distinction between Jew and Greek;
for the same Lord is Lord of all,
abounding in riches for all who call on Him; for,
"Whoever will call on the name of the Lord will be saved."
—ROMANS 10:12–13

My Task/Challenge

_____
_____
_____
_____
_____
_____
_____
_____
_____

My Outcome/Results

_____
_____
_____
_____
_____
_____
_____
_____
_____

DAY 29 ~ *He Holds the Future*

*"Remember these things, O Jacob, and Israel, for you are
My servant; I have formed you, you are My servant,
O Israel, you will not be forgotten by Me."*
—ISAIAH 44:21

*I*f those to whom God was speaking in the above verse would remember "these things," God would remember them. This promise is conditional. What "things" were they to remember? When you read Isaiah 44 in its entirety, one of those *things* becomes obvious: we are to remember the foolishness of idolatry—of relying on our ingenuity or ability to do what only God can do.

In this great oracle, God pointed out to His people the foolishness of serving idols made with hands. He compelled them to consider how silly it is to see a man plant a tree, cultivate it, chop it down, and then use the wood from that one tree to build a fire, cook a meal, and finally carve an idol for worship. The Lord called such devotion falling "before a block of wood."[139] How silly it is to worship a carved thing when we have the Lord, who made the tree, who can respond to us, who supplies us with meals and warmth, and who holds our future and eternity in His hands! All these carved images are not worthy of worship since they are merely hunks of wood.

However, that is not all the Lord stated in this great chapter. He also exposed those who practiced divination as failures and stressed the foolishness of worldly-wise men. Then, as only God can do because He knows the end from the beginning, He foretold particular details concerning a man named Cyrus:

"It is I who says of Cyrus, 'He is My shepherd! And he will perform all My desire.' And he declares of

---

[139] Isaiah 44:19

Jerusalem, 'She will be built,' and of the temple, 'Your foundation will be laid.'"[140]

Now, the only challenge for folks in that day, who must have shaken their heads at this astonishing prophecy from Isaiah, was that Jerusalem and the Temple were still standing. Besides, who was this *Cyrus* person anyway?

Cyrus would not be born for another 150 years, yet the Lord knew all about him and what he would do before he needed to do it. It is both enlightening and amazing to read the Lord's one-way conversation with Cyrus, again, 150 years before the man was even born:

> Thus says the LORD to Cyrus His anointed, whom I have taken by the right hand, to subdue nations before him and to loose the loins of kings; to open doors before him so that gates will not be shut: "I will go before you and make the rough places smooth; I will shatter the doors of bronze and cut through their iron bars. I will give you the treasures of darkness and hidden wealth of secret places; so that you may know that it is I, The LORD, the God of Israel, who calls you by your name.
>
> "For the sake of Jacob My servant, and Israel My chosen one, I have also called you by your name; I have given you a title of honor though you have not known Me. I am the LORD, and there is no other; besides Me there is no God. I will gird you, though you have not known Me; that men may know from the rising to the setting of the sun that there is no one besides Me. I am the LORD, and there is no other, the One forming light and creating darkness, causing wellbeing and creating calamity; I am the LORD who does all these."[141]

What a puzzling proclamation! To think that some guy named Cyrus, who was neither Jewish nor even born, would play such a tremendous role in something yet to come. In 586 B.C., King Nebuchadnezzar destroyed both Jerusalem and the Temple. Then, putting the worldly-wise and the diviners to shame, Cyrus, the

---

[140] Isaiah 44:28
[141] Isaiah 45:1–7

Persian king, fulfilled the prophecy in 536 B.C. after he had conquered the region, as is preserved for us in the book of Ezra.[142] It is there that we read his proclamation for the Jewish exiles to return and "rebuild the house of the LORD . . . in Jerusalem,"[143] just as the God had said he would.

Those who openly reject God are not the only ones who embarrass themselves in their attempts to divine the future or rely on power the Lord never gave them. Enter the seven sons of the Jewish priest, Sceva. These siblings attempted to have the supernatural power they saw in the life of the Apostle Paul. Unfortunately, they tried to exercise that power without the Holy Spirit living within them. They attempted to do what only God could do yet without God Himself. That never works. The outcome as they tried to exorcise a man with an evil spirit was woeful:

> And the evil spirit answered and said to them, "I recognize Jesus, and I know about Paul, but who are you?" And the man, in whom was the evil spirit, leaped on them and subdued all of them and overpowered them, so that they fled out of that house naked and wounded.[144]

Pathetic, is it not? It is always futile to attempt to do what only the Lord can do. It is just as useless to try to *appear* as if we have some hidden power or specialized knowledge about the future, as it is to be obsessed with obtaining that power or prophetic insight. The Lord knows the future, and He holds it in His precious hands. No one will thwart any of His plans, no matter what we try to predict or how we try to manipulate the outcome—even if we attempt to do so in His name.

I find it interesting that twice in today's opening verse, the Lord referred to Israel as "His servant." We are His servants as well. Before Cyrus was born, he was the Lord's unknowing servant to

---

[142] For more information on this prophecy and others, please see Norman L. Geisler, *Baker Encyclopedia of Christian Apologetics* (Grand Rapids, MI: Baker Books, 1999).
[143] Ezra 1:3
[144] Acts 19:15–16

fulfill His purposes. If a pagan king could serve God in such a way, how much more should we?

Instead of looking to idols made of wood to find purpose or human reason, or horoscopes (which many people view as "just for fun," not understanding that God forbids this), realize today that before you were born, He knew you as well. Again, if God had a clear plan and a purpose for Cyrus, a pagan king, He also has a plan for you.

Many plans are in a man's heart,
But the counsel of the LORD will stand.
—PROVERBS 19:21

My Task/Challenge

_____

_____

_____

_____

_____

_____

_____

_____

_____

_____

My Outcome/Results

_____

_____

_____

_____

_____

_____

_____

_____

_____

_____

DAY 30 ~ *God's Timing, God's Way*

"Remember the former things long past,
for I am God, and there is no other;
I am God, and there is no one like Me,
Declaring the end from the beginning,
And from ancient times things which have not been done,
Saying, 'My purpose will be established,
And I will accomplish all My good pleasure.'"
—ISAIAH 46:9–10

I don't know about you, but I am so grateful there is no god besides our God! I am so thankful there is only one true and living God Who can declare the end from the beginning, Who can call the future before an event even takes place. He is a glorious God, Who establishes and accomplishes things that have not been done before, Who acts in such miraculous ways that the only explanation can be that God Himself has intervened in individual circumstances and frailty to make something happen.

Consider the impossibility of an elderly couple who had never known the pleasure of children, who then celebrated a newborn son long after childbearing years. No wonder Sarah laughed when she heard the Lord Himself declare:

[The LORD] said, "I will surely return to you at this time next year; and behold, Sarah your wife will have a son." And Sarah was listening at the tent door, which was behind him.

Now Abraham and Sarah were old, advanced in age; Sarah was past childbearing. Sarah laughed to herself, saying, "After I have become old, shall I have pleasure, my lord being old also?"

And the LORD said to Abraham, "Why did Sarah laugh, saying, 'Shall I indeed bear a child, when I am so old?' Is anything too difficult for the LORD? At the

135

appointed time I will return to you, at this time next year, and Sarah will have a son."

Sarah denied it however, saying, "I did not laugh"; for she was afraid.

And He said, "No, but you did laugh."[145]

I think if we were honest, we'd have to admit we'd chuckle too if we stood in Sarah's sandals. Yet the Lord's answer implied the question, "Is anything too difficult for the LORD? "[146] I should say not!

Lo and behold, after a little turmoil due to a lack of faith, Isaac was born. The Lord declared the impossible and did the impossible; He established His purpose for His good pleasure with no difficulty at all. We complicate His plans for our lives with our unbelief and the manipulations we resort to when we try to make what He has clearly said He will accomplish, happen in our timing instead of His. I am so grateful He does not take our advice on what He should do or when He should do it.

Consider Peter, with his good intentions and love for the Lord Jesus. If the Lord had heeded his rebuke, our redemption would not have been possible. The drama unfolds:

> Jesus began to show His disciples that He must go to Jerusalem, and suffer many things from the elders and chief priests and scribes, and be killed, and be raised up on the third day.
>
> Peter took Him aside and began to rebuke Him, saying, "God forbid it, Lord! This shall never happen to You."
>
> But He turned and said to Peter, "Get behind Me, Satan! You are a stumbling block to Me; for you are not setting your mind on God's interests, but man's."[147]

Peter was well-intentioned, but because he did not see the end from the beginning, he had no idea that his loving desire to save

---

[145] Genesis 18:10–15
[146] Genesis 18:14
[147] Matthew 16:21–23

his beloved Friend and Master from death was also Satan's desire. This reality prompted a rather stern rebuke from our Lord: Jesus referred to Peter as *Satan* and an obstacle to God Himself!

Jesus then exposed what was at the core of Peter's rebuke. He put man's fleshly interests or desires above God's. Yet God's desire was for man's highest good, accomplished through the sacrifice of His only begotten Son. Thankfully, He established His purpose despite Peter's "Far be it from You, Lord."

So often, we think that we need to steer others toward what we believe is right or wise. Our good intentions—like Peter's, who believed Jesus should avoid the cross, or Sarah's, who thought Abraham should have a son through her handmaiden—cause us to manipulate others because we feel we need to help God in the matter. He does not need our help. He does not need our advice. We do not need to advise people to avoid the calling the Lord has for their lives, even though to us, it may seem dangerous or inconvenient. God's purposes do not need to make sense to us. That does not mean His way is nonsensical; it merely means that we need to trust in a God who has already told us, "My purpose will be established, and I will accomplish all My good pleasure."

Are you guilty of trying to talk someone out of his or her true calling? Are you refusing to support a particular missionary because they are not going where you think they should minister? Are you trying to steer a teen from military service, or to convince him or her that your alma mater or a particular branch of the military is a better door to success? Do you think that your path is the best, even if it is not the Lord's path? What about your own life—are you talking yourself out of a call of God? To sum up, are you setting your mind on man's interests or God's?

Pray about this today and ask the Lord to turn your heart to be a supportive one for His glory, no matter what the cost. Trust Him: His plan and ways are far better.

Therefore, be careful how you walk,
not as unwise men but as wise, making the most of your time,
because the days are evil. So then do not be foolish,

but understand what the will of the Lord is.
—EPHESIANS 5:15–17

My Task/Challenge

_____
_____
_____
_____
_____
_____
_____
_____
_____
_____
_____

My Outcome/Results

_____
_____
_____
_____
_____
_____
_____
_____
_____
_____
_____
_____

DAY 31 ~ *Silent No More*

But if I say, "I will not remember Him or speak anymore
in His name," then in my heart it becomes
like a burning fire shut up in my bones;
and I am weary of holding it in, and I cannot endure it.
—JEREMIAH 20:9

Today's verse points to a painful yet glorious truth. If we are called to proclaim what the Lord puts on our heart, we know that to do otherwise is not wise or worth what our conscience would endure if we kept silent even if we received a negative response.

Freshly released from the stocks, Jeremiah uttered the words above. He was beaten and bloodied for proclaiming the inconvenient Word of God to folks who not only refused to listen but would humiliate and attempt to beat him into silence. Yet their efforts were to no avail. Jeremiah continued to proclaim what the Lord placed upon his heart despite the consequences.

Just after his release, in obedience to the Lord, Jeremiah declared judgment on the very one who had the power to toss him right back into those stocks. In today's opening verse, Jeremiah lamented over the cost of proclaiming God's judgment, yet he could not resist the overwhelming and burning urge to continue regardless of the personal consequences.

Jeremiah's persistence in the presence of persecution reminds me, on a much smaller scale, of something that happened to my daughter when she was only seven years old during an outing at the lake with her grandpa one beautiful summer day. She met two little twin girls and played with them for a short time, then excitedly asked, "Do you know Jesus?"

Upon hearing the question, they began to mock her and told her to "shut up about Him." She relayed to me, calmly and matter-of-factly, that they abruptly picked up their little shovels and pails to move further down the lakeshore away from her.

I queried, "So what did you do when they went away from you?"

"I kept following them and telling them about Jesus," came her gleeful reply.

"What happened then?" I asked, thinking the exchange was over.

"Well, like I said, I kept on following them and telling them about Jesus. They didn't know Jesus," she said, in a tone as if to say, "What is wrong with you, lady? What on earth did you expect me to do?"

This little person did not give one whit about the anger those girls had toward her, or the risk she took in daring their disapproval, or the loss of getting to play with not just one little new friend but two. The important thing for her was that they did not know her Jesus. What a convicting testimony for me that day.

Peter and the disciples were in the same dilemma. Jesus had just proclaimed to them:

> "Truly, truly, I say to you, unless you eat the flesh of the Son of Man and drink His blood, you have no life in yourselves. He who eats My flesh and drinks My blood has eternal life, and I will raise him up on the last day. For My flesh is true food, and My blood is true drink.
>
> "He who eats My flesh and drinks My blood abides in Me, and I in him. As the living Father sent Me, and I live because of the Father, so he who eats Me, he also will live because of Me. This is the bread which came down out of heaven; not as the fathers ate and died; he who eats this bread will live forever."[148]

Our Lord then explained that He was referring to spiritual and not literal implications, stating, "It is the Spirit who gives life; the flesh profits nothing; the words that I have spoken to you are spirit and are life."[149] Nevertheless, "as a result of this many of His disciples withdrew and were not walking with Him anymore."

---

[148] John 6:53–58
[149] John 6:63

Seeing them leave, Jesus then asked the twelve, 'You do not want to go away also, do you?'"[150]

I love Peter's response. It is perfect for helping us to understand how a prophet like Jeremiah—or a little Nicole— would keep going under such harassment. "Simon Peter answered Him, 'Lord, to whom shall we go? You have words of eternal life. We have believed and have come to know that You are the Holy One of God.'"[151]

For us, it is the same. Because we know who Yeshua, Jesus, is, we can not keep silent. We understand that the cost to our soul and to the souls of the individuals to whom we are speaking are of greater importance than any temporary pain or suffering.

Do you see that? More importantly, do you live that? When push comes to shove, will you go away with the others, muttering to yourself that it is too hard for you to follow Jesus? Do you stand firm, despite the perceived consequences, to lovingly proclaim what you know is true and right, no matter how difficult?

Are you willing, like Jeremiah, to risk humiliation and physical suffering? Are you, like a small child, able to maintain your zeal in the face of verbal harassment? Do you feel that fire in your soul that prevents you from keeping silent? I hope so. If not, take time today and ask the Lord to give you strength despite the adversity. Commit today to speak His Word faithfully, praying for the ability to handle with grace any sort of intimidation or rejection, and allow Him to show you the victory!

For if I preach the gospel, I have nothing to boast of,
for I am under compulsion;
for woe is me if I do not preach the gospel.
—1 CORINTHIANS 9:16

---

[150] John 6:66–67
[151] John 6:68–69

My Task/Challenge

_____

_____

_____

_____

_____

_____

_____

_____

_____

_____

My Outcome/Results

_____

_____

_____

_____

_____

_____

_____

_____

_____

_____

_____

Day 32 ~ *Compassion for the Brokenhearted*

> *Surely my soul remembers and is bowed down within me.*
> *This I recall to my mind, therefore I have hope.*
> *The LORD's lovingkindnesses indeed never cease,*
> *for His compassions never fail.*
> *They are new every morning; Great is Your faithfulness.*
> —LAMENTATIONS 3:20–23

J don't think anyone in the Bible could express pain and hopelessness so well as the prophet Jeremiah, who penned the verses above. Take a moment to read Lamentations 3 and realize the depth of emotion in those verses.

It is the human condition to feel as if our time of hopelessness will never end, to feel as if all is against us. When our focus is on our temporal circumstances, those feelings become overwhelming. Perhaps we may even feel that God is against us, as Jeremiah seems to express in the first eighteen verses of this great lament.

Jeremiah was not the only person during biblical times, who felt such hopelessness. Recall the woman Naomi, who left her hometown of Bethlehem full of life and blessings but returned empty-handed, and a grieving widow and mother. Surely, she was a woman who knew that "Jeremiah moment" of feeling forsaken and forgotten by the Lord!

In the first chapter of the book of Ruth, Naomi expressed her anguish to the people of her hometown. They were astonished that the woman they once knew, who appeared to have it all, had returned broken. She lamented to her people:

> "Do not call me Naomi; call me Mara, for the Almighty has dealt very bitterly with me. I went out full, but the LORD has brought me back empty. Why do you call me Naomi, since the LORD has witnessed against me and the Almighty has afflicted me?"[152]

---

[152] Ruth 1:20–21

Yet, even as she spoke the above words, the Lord was already moving her—not only back from Moab to Bethlehem where she belonged—but also to a place of abject blessing as we witnessed on Day 7. Right under her nose, God would bring forth one of her greatest joys and blessings. She gained a daughter who would love her beyond flesh and blood and eventually a grandson in the same family line as the Messiah.

Unfortunately, Naomi's eyes were on her circumstances—her material loss and the loss of her husband and two sons—not on the greatness of God. However, it did not take long before she would again feel the Lord's blessing and hope for the future. Even the neighbor ladies recognized it. Upon the birth of Naomi's grandson Obed, to her daughter-in-law Ruth and her kinsman-redeemer, Boaz, they boldly proclaimed:

> "Blessed is the LORD who has not left you without a redeemer today, and may his name become famous in Israel. May he also be to you a restorer of life and a sustainer of your old age; for your daughter-in-law, who loves you and is better to you than seven sons, has given birth to him."
>
> Then Naomi took the child and laid him in her lap, and became his nurse. The neighbor women gave him a name, saying, "A son has been born to Naomi!" So they named him Obed. He is the father of Jesse, the father of David.[153]

What a beautiful account of changed circumstances! It was a change that began with the Lord's compassion on a broken heart. Such is the heart of Jesus, as we read of His compassion for the hurting, lost, and brokenhearted:

> Jesus was going through all the cities and villages, teaching in their synagogues and proclaiming the gospel of the kingdom, and healing every kind of disease and every kind of sickness.
>
> Seeing the people, He felt compassion for them, because they were distressed and dispirited like sheep without a shepherd. Then He said to His disciples, "The

---

[153] Ruth 4:14–17

harvest is plentiful, but the workers are few. Therefore beseech the Lord of the harvest to send out workers into His harvest."[154]

Our Lord, who is always our example, draws our focus to becoming compassionate people as well. If we learn from our Master, we will not curse our circumstances but will use them to touch others. That is not always easy. When we are in great emotional pain and feeling forsaken, we ask ourselves a myriad of questions: *Does He know how I feel? Does He see? Does He care?* However, the real question we must ask ourselves is, *Do I share His kind of compassion, and can I somehow use my pain for His glory, or am I too involved with myself to care?*

After heart-rending events in 2011 that I had never imagined I would endure, I came to a place of falling into my loving husband's arms in tears, not knowing what to do with the horrendous pain I felt. After seeking the Lord for a way to lift my sorrow, He led me to part-time work in nursing at a local assisted living and care center.

I never imagined that action would be the blessing it indeed turned out to be. By caring for others, I, the actual patient, had my heart healed. By having to study to gain specific credentials, I occupied my mind with learning something new and exciting instead of focusing on the circumstances of a broken heart and matters entirely out of my control or power to influence. The Lord opened a door for healing and blessing, and as He lifted that miserable cloud, I saw Him use me to love and touch people whom many had forgotten. In the process, He used them to heal me.

Would you be so bold as to take a step out of yourself and your circumstance to see others who may need you? Are you willing to give the Lord a chance to lift the cloud? Are you ready to take responsibility for letting the cloud linger longer than intended? Is it time to cast off the pity party and enter into the life the Lord has for you?

Reflect on this today. Pray that the Lord will show you an open door for that ray of hope to shine your way. You may see it

---

[154] Matthew 9:35–38

reflected in the people around you, who love and stand by you, or in strangers who need Yeshua's compassionate touch.

When the Lord saw her,
He felt compassion for her, and said to her,
"Do not weep."
—LUKE 7:13

My Task/Challenge

_____
_____
_____
_____
_____
_____
_____
_____
_____
_____

My Outcome/Results

_____
_____
_____
_____
_____
_____
_____
_____
_____
_____

DAY 33 ~ *When Sin Finds You Out*

> *"You will remember your ways and all your deeds with which you have defiled yourselves; and you will loathe yourselves in your own sight for all the evil things that you have done. Then you will know that I am the LORD when I have dealt with you for My name's sake, not according to your evil ways or according to your corrupt deeds, O house of Israel," declares the Lord God.*
> —EZEKIEL 20:43–44

zekiel's prophecy in the passage above relating to Israel's return to the Lord and their utter heartbrokenness at the memory of their sin and rebellion brings to my mind events in the book of Joshua. There, Israel faced an easy win against the small city of Ai. A few spies advised Joshua that he did not need to send the whole army to battle, but rather just two or three thousand men to take care of the pesky problem that was Ai. However, because one man disobeyed God's command, Israel received an unexpected trouncing. The seemingly secret sin of Achan affected everyone and cost many their lives. The price of sin is high.

The interesting thing is that the Lord Himself could have immediately called out Achan for stealing what was under the ban. He did not. The morning after the tragic battle loss, there would be a process of narrowing down the people to expose the culprit. Tribes narrowed down to families and families to one family in particular, then down to the individual himself. Yes, there Achan stood, with a *"What who me?"* expression on his face. Through that narrowing and harrowing process, he'd thought he just might get away with it. He never stepped up on his own; he did not take responsibility until he was the only one left.

It is easy to be contrite when finally caught. Confronted, Achan confessed:

> "Truly, I have sinned against the LORD, the God of Israel, and this is what I did: When I saw among the spoil a beautiful mantle from Shinar and two hundred shekels

of silver and a bar of gold fifty shekels in weight, then I coveted them and took them; and behold, they are concealed in the earth inside my tent with the silver underneath it."[155]

Once the sin was exposed, once the sinner was dealt with, victory came to Israel. However, those who witnessed the exposure of Achan's sin never forgot that powerful lesson. I imagine it heightened their awe of a God who truly sees and holds us accountable. He taught them that the sin of one affects the many, and the only remedy is full confession and genuine repentance.

What would have happened if Achan had come to Joshua while Joshua was still on his knees, crying out to the Lord after their failure at Ai? What would have happened had Achan, while clutching those stolen goods, touched his shoulder as Joshua knelt there and made that same confession? The Lord certainly gave him plenty of time. Perhaps instead of condemnation, he would have heard the words, "Go, and sin no more."

If only Achan had the broken heart of our opening verse before he had to be exposed! True repentance prompts brokenness over the memory of our sin and gratitude to the One who can remove its penalty.

Such was the case of a certain woman in the gospel of Luke:

> Now one of the Pharisees was requesting Him [Jesus] to dine with him, and He entered the Pharisee's house and reclined at the table. And there was a woman in the city who was a sinner; and when she learned that He was reclining at the table in the Pharisee's house, she brought an alabaster vial of perfume, and standing behind Him at His feet, weeping, she began to wet His feet with her tears, and kept wiping them with the hair of her head, and kissing His feet and anointing them with the perfume.
>
> Now when the Pharisee who had invited Him saw this, he said to himself, "If this man were a prophet He

---

[155] Joshua 7:20–21

would know who and what sort of person this woman is who is touching Him, that she is a sinner."[156]

Jesus was well aware of who the woman was and what she had done. More importantly, the woman knew who she was and what she had done. Her very posture is the evidence for this, as she cleaned Yeshua's feet and shed tears of loss, regret, and undying love—as she took the most precious thing she possessed and offered it in such a humble, beautiful, grateful manner. Yet those who thought they were okay with God never heard the words from Jesus that she did: "Your sins have been forgiven," and "Your faith has saved you; go in peace."[157]

This repentant woman, who remembered her sins and was sorrowful for them, heard those words of forgiveness from the only Person in that room who would and could proclaim them. All the Pharisees could do was judge her and neglect to see the sin in their hearts. In the process, they neglected to give their Messiah one-eighth of the honor she expressed toward Him. As a result, they received a deserved rebuke; she received forgiveness and eternal life.

Like Achan or the Pharisees, we think God will not see our sin if we hide it. We tend to hide it even from ourselves. However, as they learned, this does not do us any good. When we admit our sin, confess it, and are truly heartbroken, remembering the pain we have brought to the heart of our Lord and often to others, we move to a place of repentance with the knowledge that our sins are forgiven.

The truth is that the more we try to hide it, the more we will see and feel the consequences of our sin around us. Are there a few "secret sins" in your life that are not secrets to the Lord? What about the sin of gluttony? You may be unwilling even to admit this is a sin, but your type 2 diabetes, your heart disease, and your high blood pressure have all found you out; they all expose your overindulgence.

Are you surfing the net where you should not be? There is a reason they named it the World Wide *Web*. Have you been

---

[156] Luke 7:36–39
[157] Luke 7:48, 50

engaging in playful conversations, "innocently," with old friends of the opposite sex on social networking websites? Are you a young person who imagines that "everyone is doing it" or that "if it feels good, it must be okay," so it is okay for you to push the boundaries of sexual purity as well?

Do you imagine that your Guy or Gal Smiley routine among the congregation masks your out-of-control temper at home? Do you think these things do not affect others in the camp, under your roof, in your fellowship, or elsewhere? Well, they do.

If you do not have the heartfelt sorrow over sin, as expressed in the opening verse today, you must ask yourself why not. Seek the Lord in these matters. Ask Him to reveal what hinders your relationship with Him and others, and then fall at His feet like the woman with the alabaster vial.

Why should any living mortal, or any man,
offer complaint in view of his sins?
Let us examine and probe our ways,
and let us return to the LORD.
—LAMENTATIONS 3:39–40

My Task/Challenge

_____
_____
_____
_____
_____
_____
_____
_____
_____
_____

My Outcome/Results

_____
_____
_____
_____
_____
_____
_____
_____
_____
_____
_____

DAY 34 ~ *The Lure of Compromise*

> *"My people, remember now what Balak King of Moab counseled and what Balaam son of Beor answered him, and from Shittim to Gilgal, so that you might know the righteous acts of the LORD."*
> —MICAH 6:5

The backdrop to today's opening verse is Numbers 22–24, where we read about old King Balak, whose feared enemies the Israelites, had routed their foes and were now only a stone's throw away.

Balak decided to send messengers, with cash in hand, to beg a well-known diviner named Balaam to curse God's people. After a little time of haggling with Balaam, whom God distinctly told *not* to curse the people, Balak's messengers prevailed in convincing Balaam to saddle his donkey and go back with them to meet with Balak. Balaam's mind was on a pending fortune, not on God's command to bless the people rather than curse them.

His donkey, having more spiritual insight than his master did, saw the Angel of the Lord standing in its way to prevent him from going further. In Balaam's angry outburst, he struck the donkey three times. Thus, a conversation ensued between Balaam, the donkey, and the Angel of the Lord. Balaam needed another reminder to get his eyes off his agenda and be sure to communicate only what the Lord told him to.

The result of all this was a blessing times three in Israel's favor. Balak was not pleased. Nevertheless, Balaam figured out a way to gain the cash after all, because the next event we read, after Balaam returned home, is a tragic one:

> While Israel remained at Shittim, the people began to play the harlot with the daughters of Moab. For they invited the people to the sacrifices of their gods, and the people ate and bowed down to their gods. So Israel

joined themselves to Baal of Peor, and the LORD was angry against Israel.[158]

Israel's participation in idolatry and the corrupt rites associated with the worship of Baal-peor were directly attributed to the influence of that one man. Israel unceremoniously killed Balaam, along with the five kings of Midian, as outlined in Numbers 31. Balaam had figured out a way to help Midia without speaking a word against Israel. He would simply tempt Israel to bring corruption into their camp.

Balaam is not the only one we read about in God's Word, who allowed wealth to entice a change in allegiance. Judas, who pilfered from Jesus's money box, thought thirty pieces of silver a fair exchange for his betrayal of Him to the chief priests of Israel. [159]

Greed got the better of Judas. He never imagined the outcome would lead to the death of the One he had betrayed. Perhaps he thought that by turning Jesus over to the chief priests, he would just gain a little cash and distance himself from a man he thought had gone over the line with His teaching. Maybe he hoped Jesus would be silenced or forced to move to another country with His wild proclamations of being Savior and Son of God. I think this because of the immediate reaction of Judas when he realized where his dirty deed lead Jesus—right to Calvary's cross. Yet the paths for Messiah and betrayer were irreversible:

> Then when Judas, who had betrayed Him, saw that He had been condemned, he felt remorse and returned the thirty pieces of silver to the chief priests and elders, saying, "I have sinned by betraying innocent blood."
>
> But they said, "What is that to us? See to that yourself!" And he threw the pieces of silver into the temple sanctuary and departed; and he went away and hanged himself.[160]

We never really know the horror or extent of our compromise until the wheels are in motion, the deed is accomplished, and it is too late to reverse course. I know two

---

[158] Numbers 25:1–3
[159] John 12:4–6
[160] Matthew 27:3–5

pastors who served the Lord well for years but became enticed by their flesh and found themselves, literal prisoners, leaving their families devastated and humiliated and their congregations reeling.

We have all seen what financial greed can do to prominent ministry leaders who begin with good intentions but allow the almighty dollar to replace Almighty God on the throne of their lives.

However, what about the individual who is not so well known? What about that hidden place in our hearts that we imagine won't matter since no one else knows? If we ever begin to believe that compromise with sin and the world is no big deal, we have just taken Balaam's counsel, and like Judas, we have betrayed our Lord in exchange for something temporal.

Are you on the verge of such a compromise? Is someone whispering in your ear the sweet nothings of wealth, fame, or physical satisfaction that are distracting you from doing what is right before the Lord, your family, and your community?

Stop now—today. Decide to put that temptation away and replace it with the power of God's Word and His promises to those who persevere in the face of temptation. You will soon find that each time you turn away from compromise, claiming the Word of God for your strength, the less of a hold this area of temptation will have on your thought life. You know what you have to do. Do not hesitate to do it today.

"But I have a few things against you, because you have there some who hold the teaching of Balaam, who kept teaching Balak to put a stumbling block before the sons of Israel, to eat things sacrificed to idols and to commit acts of immorality . . . Therefore repent."
—REVELATION 2:14, 16

My Task/Challenge

_____
_____
_____
_____
_____
_____
_____
_____
_____
_____

My Outcome/Results

_____
_____
_____
_____
_____
_____
_____
_____
_____
_____
_____

DAY 35 ~ *His Building Plan*

Thus says the LORD of hosts, "Consider your ways!"
—HAGGAI 1:7

The prophet Haggai spoke during an event that sparked the people of Israel to look inward at their priorities and zeal for the Lord's work. A small remnant of Jews had left Babylonian exile to return to Jerusalem and rebuild the Temple. A mission that began with zeal ended with discouragement and faded into the distraction of their daily, personal existence. For approximately sixteen years, God's unfinished house collected dust as the remnant went about building their lives instead of the Temple.

Suddenly, the Lord spoke through the prophet Haggai to point the finger at the reason why the people never felt as if they could ever prosper:

"Thus says the LORD of hosts, 'This people says, "The time has not come, even the time for the house of the LORD to be rebuilt."'"

Then the word of the LORD came by Haggai the prophet, saying, "Is it time for you yourselves to dwell in your paneled houses while this house lies desolate?"

Now therefore, thus says the LORD of hosts, "Consider your ways! You have sown much, but harvest little; you eat, but there is not enough to be satisfied; you drink, but there is not enough to become drunk; you put on clothing, but no one is warm enough; and he who earns, earns wages to put into a purse with holes."

Thus says the LORD of hosts, "Consider your ways! Go up to the mountains, bring wood and rebuild the temple, that I may be pleased with it and be glorified," says the LORD. "You look for much, but behold, it comes to little; when you bring it home, I blow it away. Why?"

declares the LORD of hosts, "Because of My house which lies desolate, while each of you runs to his own house."[161]

Working at cross-purposes with God is the ultimate in spinning your wheels! The Jewish remnant needed to get the Lord's work done, and *time was a-wastin'*! Because of discouragement and the overwhelming challenge they faced, they preferred to concentrate on their own needs. They did not realize that the Lord meets our needs when we are obedient to do the inconvenient and sometimes frustrating tasks that fulfilling His will might require. There was a bigger picture than their mundane lives at stake, and they needed to see it.

While the remnant lost the zeal to build, we fast-forward in time to see someone else who was very eager to build something for the Lord:

> Jesus took with Him Peter, and James, and John, and brought them up on a high mountain by themselves. And He was transfigured before them; and His garments became radiant and exceedingly white, as no launderer on earth can whiten them. Elijah appeared to them along with Moses; and they were talking with Jesus.
>
> Peter said to Jesus, "Rabbi, it is good for us to be here; let us make three tabernacles, one for You, and one for Moses, and one for Elijah." For he did not know what to answer; for they became terrified.
>
> Then a cloud formed, overshadowing them, and a voice came out of the cloud, "This is My beloved Son, listen to Him!"[162]

Peter had good intentions, but he was shortsighted. In his mind, this mountain moment was the pinnacle experience, and he felt that piece of real estate needed a few tabernacles to transform it into a primary place of worship.

As is usually the case, a little correction was in order. Peter did not know the implications of his desire to build because, once again, he did not have God's perspective. His motivation was from

---

[161] Haggai 1:2–9
[162] Mark 9:2–7

a place of fearful awe. The Father was gracious to step in and put the focus where it needed to be—and that was not on the temporal.

Instead, Peter's focus needed to be on listening to—walking in absolute obedience to—Jesus and His Word. *"Listen to Him."* That was the message for the other disciples who were with him as well. *"Guys, don't take Peter's advice on this one. Keep following the command of the Supreme Commander."*

Zeal for the Lord is not the only thing required for service. Many people think it is and become frustrated over a lack of fruit in their particular ministry despite their passion. So often, they give up on the work because, like the remnant that started well, they get discouraged with the process. Like Peter, their efforts are sometimes in the wrong task.

That leads to today's questions. Where are you in your zeal for the Lord's work and following His will to accomplish it? Do you find yourself discouraged? Are you spinning your wheels? Have you completely abandoned the task for various reasons or excuses and thus have unwittingly adjusted your focus to the temporal? Today's opening verse is for all. "Consider your ways!"

Are you doing things your way, or are you seeking the Lord's way for your calling? Neither run ahead nor drag your feet or get discouraged. Confirm His will in the work you do in His name. Put it all out before Him today and ask Him for guidance, direction, and an open door. He is faithful. He desires that you follow His will. Therefore, He will be faithful to answer.

However, the Most High does not dwell in houses made by human hands; as the prophet says:
"HEAVEN IS MY THRONE, AND EARTH
IS THE FOOTSTOOL OF MY FEET;
WHAT KIND OF HOUSE WILL YOU BUILD FOR ME?" *says the Lord,*
"OR WHAT PLACE IS THERE FOR MY REPOSE?"
—ACTS 7:48–49

My Task/Challenge

_____
_____
_____
_____
_____
_____
_____
_____
_____
_____

My Outcome/Results

_____
_____
_____
_____
_____
_____
_____
_____
_____
_____

DAY 36 ~ *Faith and Sacrifice*

"Consider the ravens, for they neither sow nor reap; they have no storeroom nor barn, and yet God feeds them; how much more valuable you are than the birds!"
—LUKE 12:24

onsider the ravens, indeed! Elijah was subject to the same drought that was brought upon King Ahab by the Lord and that Elijah proclaimed. The Lord provided for Elijah during that drought, using a brook for drink and ravens to bring him bread and meat every morning and evening. Nevertheless, eventually, the brook dried up. Was that it? Would that be the end of God's provision for Elijah?

Absolutely not! Through additional provision for Elijah, the Lord also spared a widow and her starving son in Zarephath from certain death. The Lord directed Elijah to make a little request of that faithful and certainly hungry and sorrowful mom:

"Please get me a little water in a jar, that I may drink." As she was going to get it, he called to her and said, "Please bring me a piece of bread in your hand."

But she said, "As the LORD your God lives, I have no bread, only a handful of flour in the bowl and a little oil in the jar; and behold, I am gathering a few sticks that I may go in and prepare for me and my son, that we may eat it and die."

Then Elijah said to her, "Do not fear; go, do as you have said, but make me a little bread cake from it first and bring it out to me, and afterward you may make one for yourself and for your son. For thus says the LORD God of Israel, 'The bowl of flour shall not be exhausted, nor shall the jar of oil be empty, until the day that the LORD sends rain on the face of the earth.'"

So she went and did according to the word of Elijah, and she and he and her household ate for many days.

162

The bowl of flour was not exhausted nor did the jar of oil become empty, according to the word of the LORD which He spoke through Elijah.[163]

Jehovah-Jireh—The Lord Provides. Not only did God meet Elijah's need, but He also provided for the woman's household. He cares more for the individual who hungers and thirsts than He does for the ravens that He used to provide for Elijah. As our opening verse declared, birds aren't pacing their nests, saying, "What are we going to eat today?" The Lord provides for their need exactly when they need it. Therefore He will surely meet ours.

Consider not only the ravens but also a little boy with five barley loaves and two fish who was willing to give them up to Jesus so He could use them as He saw fit.[164] What a wise decision! The lad's tummy was satisfied as a result, as were five thousand other people's, with twelve full baskets to spare. What an excellent investment that boy made.

These blessings both took an act of faith and sacrifice. I love how that mother did not think twice about giving Elijah what he requested, even though her sacrifice could have meant impending death for her and her beloved son. However, I must say something about Elijah's trust and faith, as well. Did you notice that he did not argue with God when he was to proclaim a drought? Elijah did not say, "Wait a minute, that's going to affect me too! Can't we resort to the sore boils thing?" Instead, he declared the word of the Lord and trusted God to care for him.

I also appreciate how the boy in the feeding of the five thousand did not hesitate to give every bit of his personal provision to Jesus. The great work, the lives saved in each account, required faith and sacrifice. Why should we be surprised? Our eternal provision required faith and sacrifice, as well.

What about you? Are you clinging to what the Lord would like you to release so He can use it for His purposes? Are your knuckles white from how tight you clutch the things of this world rather than giving them up for the kingdom? Are you afraid that if

---

[163] 1 Kings 17:10–16
[164] John 6:1–14

you give something up, when your time of need comes, there will not be any provision for you?

I am not advocating that you sell everything you have and give it to the poor. That might be a specific call for some, but it is not a command of God for all people. What I am suggesting is that it is okay to release by faith what you tightly grasp because you are afraid that the Lord won't meet your need if you let it go.

I imagine there are many people in the world whom the Lord would love to use in feeding of five thousand, but instead of being part of a miracle, they would rather not loosen their grip. Pray about this. Remember, if God feeds the birds, He is going to supply for you. Do not be afraid to let go of your last little fish, or a loaf of bread, or a bit of flour. Release it to Him if He has called you to do that, and enjoy being part of His multiplication miracle.

"But I would feed you with the finest of the wheat,
And with honey from the rock I would satisfy you."
—PSALM 81:16

My Task/Challenge

My Outcome/Results

DAY 37 ~ *Clothed in Humility*

"Consider the lilies, how they grow: they neither toil nor spin; but I tell you, not even Solomon in all his glory clothed himself like one of these. But if God so clothes the grass in the field, which is alive today and tomorrow is thrown into the furnace, how much more will He clothe you? You men of little faith!"
—LUKE 12:27–28

The first mention of clothing in the Scriptures is found in the book of Genesis. We find it in the account of Adam and Eve with eyes opened, sin exposed, and a flood of fear and shame overwhelming them. In a pathetic attempt to cover their sin and shame, they decided to clothe themselves by sewing leaves together. These first garments proved insufficient. The Lord knew they needed a more appropriate coverage for their shame. "The LORD God made garments of skin for Adam and his wife, and clothed them."[165]

What the Lord clothed Adam and Eve with did not come with designer labels. Those first outfits were not glittery and fancy. There certainly was nothing to boast about in wearing them, no reason to strut around. The fact that these skins were covering their bodies was a reminder that they lost their innocence due to pride and willful disobedience. No, the Lord God provided what was functional for the harsh conditions they would soon confront, and they were of much stronger material than that of leaves.

In the clothing process, God also instituted the sacrificial system. For the first time, Adam and Eve would witness death, the shedding of blood, to cover sin. They had a firsthand look at the horrible price of their disobedience. I imagine a sense of their mortality hit them as they witnessed a fellow creature of flesh and blood die. They fully understood that just as God had said, they too would meet physical death.

---

[165] Genesis 3:21

This first shedding of blood must have been a painful experience on another level. Since Adam named the animals, he must have had an extraordinary relationship with them. I know that any animal I name is, from that point on, my pet. Now, here they were, clothed with a dead animal's skin. Daily they carried the reminder upon their bodies of the consequences for disregarding God's clear warning. Even so, in the face of their disobedience, God provided an appropriate sacrifice to cover their sin and shame. He clothed them.

In Revelation 3, our Lord Jesus, to the congregation in Laodicea, offers a stern warning that is appropriate for us today:

> "I know your deeds, that you are neither cold nor hot; I wish that you were cold or hot. So because you are lukewarm, and neither hot nor cold, I will spit you out of My mouth. Because you say, 'I am rich, and have become wealthy, and have need of nothing,' and you do not know that you are wretched and miserable and poor and blind and naked, I advise you to buy from Me gold refined by fire so that you may become rich, and white garments so that you may clothe yourself, and that the shame of your nakedness will not be revealed; and eye salve to anoint your eyes so that you may see. Those whom I love, I reprove and discipline; therefore be zealous and repent."[166]

Laodicea was a wealthy community. There, at the temple of Asclepius, a medical school had advanced a special eye salve that healed common eye infections or diseases of that region. It appears that the members of this congregation beautifully adorned themselves because they had the finances to do so.

The Laodiceans did not feel it necessary to rely on God. They were so impressed in their own eyes with their ability to clothe themselves exquisitely, but because of their apathy and pride, they did not realize that in the Lord's eyes, they were stark naked. The truth was that the only One who could clothe them properly was the Lord Yeshua Himself.

---

[166] Revelation 3:15–19

How sad to realize that the sign of our shame has become a point of pride! From the designer tags on our clothes to the prices on those tags, we become like the Laodiceans. We tie our identity to what we can afford and, unfortunately, more frequently, what we can't.

What is even more tragic is that many of us teach our children to view clothing in the same way. We have placed our worth in fancy clothes and high price tags. Yet the truth is that clothing is something we now must have because we carry sin and shame in a fallen world with harsh elements. Talk about a loss of focus.

On the other hand, some profess to trust in the Lord but do not believe He will provide for their basic need of clothing, as Jesus pointed out in today's opening verse. However, His was a twofold promise. Not only *will* He, *has* He and *does* He provide for our physical need of clothing, but He has also covered our sin and shame as well.

Assess your heart today. Do you worry that you simply will not have what is appropriate to meet your true needs? Alternatively, do you flaunt your wealth by what you wear? Do you teach your children to do the same? Do your children feel stress at the perception that they will not have proper clothing to keep them warm in winter, or are they hounding you because the name on the tag dangling from their garments is unknown to their friends?

Trust the Lord in this area to clothe you appropriately, both inside and out. Then look forward to exchanging every article of clothing you own for the one that truly awaits you.

"Let us rejoice and be glad and give the glory to Him,
for the marriage of the Lamb has come
and His bride has made herself ready."
It was given to her to clothe herself in fine linen,
bright and clean; for the fine linen is the righteous acts of the saints.
—REVELATION 19:7–8

My Task/Challenge

_____
_____
_____
_____
_____
_____
_____
_____
_____
_____

My Outcome/Results

_____
_____
_____
_____
_____
_____
_____
_____
_____
_____
_____

DAY 38 ~ *No Looking Back*

"Remember Lot's wife."
—LUKE 17:32

W hat an ominous reminder. The above text points to a stunning and dramatic event in Genesis, one that is hard to forget. It is a reference to something that happened during the judgment upon the cities of Sodom and Gomorrah.

The account is stomach-turning. We imagine people who were so corrupt; there were not even ten righteous individuals living among those cities.[167] Can we blame God for judging such wicked places? However, there was another judgment our Lord would like us to remember—one that happened to an individual who refused to heed a specific warning.

As two angels led the hesitant crew of Lot, his unnamed wife, and his two daughters out of Sodom to escape the imminent judgment, one of the angels communicated two specific warnings: "Escape for your life! Do not look behind you."[168]

The family's original hesitancy to leave such a depraved place—a place where the men of the city threatened to break into Lot's house to "act wickedly" against the angels who visited them—is pretty shocking when you think of it. I imagine any of us would say, "I am so thankful God is plucking me out of such a debauched city!" However, that was not the case for Lot and the ladies. Astoundingly, despite the warning from one of the angels to keep her eyes forward no matter what, the temptation to look back proved too great for Lot's wife.

Then the LORD rained on Sodom and Gomorrah brimstone and fire from the LORD out of heaven, and He overthrew those cities, and all the valley, and all the inhabitants of the cities, and what grew on the ground.

[167] Genesis 18:32
[168] Genesis 19:17

But his wife, from behind him, looked back, and she became a pillar of salt.[169]

We can speculate until the cows come home as to why she looked back. Was it a longing look? Did she feel she was going to miss her friends and possessions? Did she enjoy the energy that came with such an environment? Or perhaps she had hated every moment of living there and wanted to see those wicked people get what was coming to them. All we know from the actual account is that she disobeyed.

The words of our Lord surrounding today's verse may end our speculation. Reading the Scriptures in context is extremely important, and it serves us well in the case of Lot's wife. Since our Lord knows every human heart, He certainly knew hers. The Lord Jesus, in a discussion regarding another time of judgment, one still yet to come, warned:

> "It was the same as happened in the days of Lot: they were eating, they were drinking, they were buying, they were selling, they were planting, they were building; but on the day that Lot went out from Sodom it rained fire and brimstone from heaven and destroyed them all.
>
> "It will be just the same on the day that the Son of Man is revealed. On that day, the one who is on the housetop and whose goods are in the house must not go down to take them out; and likewise the one who is in the field must not turn back. Remember Lot's wife. Whoever seeks to keep his life will lose it, and whoever loses his life will preserve it."[170]

According to Jesus, Mrs. Lot's look back was indeed one of longing for the old life, for her stuff, for the familiarity she had built amid utter wickedness. Her impulsive and compulsive desire to look back was greater than her desire to obey the angel's command.

Can you relate to Lot's wife? Is your life here and now so comfortable that you would say, "Just let me pack a few things first."? If the Lord sent an angel to grab you by the wrist to high-

[169] Genesis 19:24–26
[170] Luke 17:28–33

tail it out of your cozy environment, would *you* longingly look back?

It is death to cling to anything of this world in such a way that it hardens us to the truth of what will ultimately become of our stuff; it is death to look back in such a way that we lose sight of where our true treasures lie.

There is nothing wrong with a healthy look at our past. However, we are to look longingly forward to what awaits us. We are to look expectantly and excitedly for "the day when the Son of Man is revealed."[171] We want to remember His coming, not the way we lived before we knew Him. The only time we need to look back is to recount God's goodness in our lives—but never to look back longingly as Lot's wife.

Is there a time in your life that you long to relive? Do you have a desire to go back to those "good ole days"? Perhaps you do not realize that pressing on toward the prize that is in Yeshua, our Savior, is where the blessings flow.[172] Just perhaps, if you are still looking longingly to your past, you are missing the fact that greater works of His are ahead of you. Leave it behind you. Do not look back. Daily be conformed to the image of His Son.[173] Since you were less conformed in your past, it's better to leave it there.

Jesus said, "No one, after putting his hand to the plow and looking back, is fit for the kingdom of God."
—LUKE 9:62

---

[171] Like 17:30
[172] Philippians 3:14
[173] Romans 8:29

My Task/Challenge

_____
_____
_____
_____
_____
_____
_____
_____
_____
_____

My Outcome/Results

_____
_____
_____
_____
_____
_____
_____
_____
_____
_____
_____

DAY 39 ~ *The Suffering Servant*

*"He is not here, but He has risen. Remember how
He spoke to you while He was still in Galilee, saying that the
Son of Man must be delivered into the hands of sinful men, and be
crucified, and the third day rise again."
And they remembered His words.*
—LUKE 24:6–8

They had gone to the tomb with spices and perfume to anoint Jesus's body—"Mary Magdalene and Joanna and Mary the mother of James; also the other women with them."[174] To their surprise, the enormous stone that had once covered the tomb was rolled away. Upon entering, they realized His body was gone. Even more to their dismay, they beheld two men in dazzling clothing, who said to them, "Why do you seek the living One among the dead?"[175] The *men* then spoke the words of our opening passage.

The men in dazzling clothing seemed puzzled as to why the women would be looking for Jesus in the tomb. Had the women not heard what Jesus prophesied concerning His suffering, death, burial, and resurrection?

> "Behold, we are going up to Jerusalem, and all things which are written through the prophets about the Son of Man will be accomplished. For He will be handed over to the Gentiles, and will be mocked and mistreated and spit upon, and after they have scourged Him, they will kill Him; and the third day He will rise again."[176]

Not only had Jesus specifically communicated what would happen to Him, but the prophets foretold these events hundreds of years before they took place! God made sure nothing would be

---

[174] Luke 24:10
[175] Luke 24:4–5
[176] Luke 18:31–33

lost or misunderstood. No wonder the angels were puzzled by the women's actions!

Many eye-opening and specific prophecies foretold of the Messiah's betrayal and arrest. Scripture tells us He would be mocked, mistreated, spat upon, scourged, and crucified. Regarding the betrayal, Psalm 41:9 reads, "Even my close friend in whom I trusted, who ate my bread, has lifted up his heel against me."

Regarding those individuals who would mock Him, Psalm 22:6–8 states:

> But I am a worm and not a man, a reproach of men and despised by the people. All who see me sneer at me; they separate with the lip, they wag the head, saying, "Commit yourself to the LORD; let Him deliver him; let Him rescue him, because He delights in him."

Isaiah 50:6 records, "I gave My back to those who strike Me, and My cheeks to those who pluck out the beard; I did not cover My face from humiliation and spitting."

Psalm 22:11–14 is an accurate description of what Yeshua suffered when crucified:

> I am poured out like water, and all my bones are out of joint; my heart is like wax; it is melted within me. My strength is dried up like a potsherd, and my tongue cleaves to my jaws; and You lay me in the dust of death.
>
> For dogs have surrounded me; a band of evildoers has encompassed me; they pierced my hands and my feet. I can count all my bones. They look, they stare at me; they divide my garments among them, and for my clothing they cast lots.

Not only do we find in the Old Covenant Scriptures that and how the Messiah would die, but the prophet Isaiah also offered the answer as to why. If we only had Isaiah 53 to check Jesus's prophecy regarding Himself, it would be plenty to prove the validity of the Scriptures concerning Him:

> But He was pierced through for our transgressions, He was crushed for our iniquities; the chastening for our well-being fell upon Him, and by His scourging we are

healed. All of us like sheep have gone astray, Each of us has turned to his own way; but the LORD has caused the iniquity of us all to fall on Him . . .

His grave was assigned with wicked men, yet He was with a rich man in His death, because He had done no violence, nor was there any deceit in His mouth. But the LORD was pleased to crush Him, putting Him to grief; if He would render Himself as a guilt offering . . .

As a result of the anguish of His soul, He will see it and be satisfied; by His knowledge the Righteous One, My Servant, will justify the many, as He will bear their iniquities. Therefore, I will allot Him a portion with the great, and He will divide the booty with the strong; because He poured out Himself to death, and was numbered with the transgressors; yet He Himself bore the sin of many, and interceded for the transgressors.[177]

Lastly, regarding the three days after His crucifixion, Jesus prophesied:

An evil and adulterous generation craves for a sign; and yet no sign will be given to it but the sign of Jonah the prophet; for just as Jonah was three days and three nights in the belly of the sea monster, so will the Son of Man be three days and three nights in the heart of the earth.[178]

Everything Jesus and the prophets before Him prophesied regarding His birth, life, death, burial, and resurrection came true. We can rely upon Him and His eternal Word. However, the focus for me here is that Jesus knowingly faced every bit of the horror He endured for us. No wonder His sweat was as drops of blood in the garden the night of the betrayal. He knew the tortuous death He would experience, the forsaking by the very ones He came to save, and the weight of guilt and shame, of all humanity, upon Himself.

What an amazing, compassionate, longsuffering Lord we serve! Have you contemplated this lately? Have you taken time to

---

[177] Isaiah 53:5–6, 9–10a,11–12
[178] Matthew 12:39–40

consider all He endured for you? Have you given Him adequate thanks and praise for this fact? If it has been a while, take time to kneel before Him today and truly thank Him for all He suffered for you.

The LORD says to my Lord: "Sit at My right hand until I make Your enemies a footstool for Your feet."
—PSALM 110:1

My Task/Challenge

_____
_____
_____
_____
_____
_____
_____
_____
_____
_____

My Outcome/Results

_____
_____
_____
_____
_____
_____
_____
_____
_____
_____
_____

DAY 40 ~ *Facing Persecution*

"Remember the word that I said to you,
'A slave is not greater than his master.'
If they persecuted Me, they will also persecute you;
if they kept My word, they will keep yours also."
—JOHN 15:20

hroughout history, there is a recognition for the principle of identification with the master that Jesus warned us about in the opening passage for today. That would include an account concerning the children of Israel. As long as Pharaoh and his Egypt benefited from one particular son of Jacob, namely Joseph, who helped them survive a seven-year famine, all would be right with the world for Israel. However, when time passed, hatred for God became a hatred for God's people.

Pharaoh had no problem taking counsel from Joseph, a man whose God was as far from his Egyptian deities as possible. After all, Pharaoh knew who buttered his bread. The wise counsel of Joseph, who relied upon his God, made Pharaoh even more renowned during the time of famine. He did not even mind if Jacob's entire family came to live in a neighboring community and benefitted as well. All seemed harmonious —*until.*

Significant time passed. Israel grew greater in number. They were blessed and abundant. After a while, the celebrated events of Joseph helping the Egyptians survive the horrible famine became a lost memory. There was a new Pharaoh in town who decided to turn them into slaves. The Scriptures reveal that the Egyptians "appointed taskmasters over them to afflict them with hard labor. And they built for Pharaoh storage cities, Pithom and Raamses."[179]

However, the God of Israel was not deaf to their cries for help. Therefore, He decided to use the unlikely "slow of speech

---

[179] Exodus 1:11

and slow of tongue"[180] Moses to ask Pharaoh to let the people go into the wilderness for sacrifice to and worship of their God.

> Moses and Aaron came and said to Pharaoh, "Thus says the LORD, the God of Israel, 'Let My people go that they may celebrate a feast to Me in the wilderness.'"

> But Pharaoh said, "Who is the LORD that I should obey His voice to let Israel go? I do not know the LORD, and besides, I will not let Israel go."[181]

If Pharaoh did not respect the Lord God and His will, he certainly was not going to respect His representative. Thus, Pharaoh's disrespect led to even more intense persecution of the Hebrews; their labor became harder, and the thrashings increased.

Nevertheless, that was not the end of the story. God stepped in and used Moses to deliver His people. So great was the deliverance that those Hebrew slaves did not leave like paupers. They departed with the riches of Egypt in their hands. Yet, even though they lived through this great victory, plundered the Egyptians, and watched the swallowing up of Pharaoh's entire army in the Red Sea, they too showed their disregard for God repeatedly throughout their wilderness journey. And as much as the children of Israel grumbled against God, they also grumbled against Moses.

Jesus reminded all who heard Him speak, and later those who would read His words, that the slave is not greater than his master is. Those who decide to call Him Lord and Master must keep in mind that if individuals persecuted Him, we who follow Him should expect persecution as well.

Indeed, we realize the horrible nature of the abuse He endured, as we saw on Day 39 of this devotional book. Those who hated Jesus persecuted Him to the point of crucifixion. In John 16:2–3, Jesus stated plainly, "An hour is coming for everyone who kills you to think that he is offering service to God. These things they will do because they have not known the Father or Me." When we share the gospel, we don't often mention this to the folks with whom we witness.

---

[180] Exodus 4:10
[181] Exodus 5:1–2

However, what would happen if followers of Yeshua embraced this expectation of trouble and cast off their concern about persecution? Some believers in the United States think if someone merely shuns or laughs at them, that is persecution. In many countries around the world, our brothers and sisters are losing their lives because those who kill them think they are doing God a favor. Yet, willingly and obediently, those faithful missionaries go.

What about you? Do you consider an old friend not returning your phone call because he doesn't want to be anywhere near a "Jesus freak" persecution? Do you believe it's persecution when someone at your work asks you to remove your *"Jesus is the Reason for the Season"* pin? Are you surprised when trouble of any kind comes your way because of your beliefs? Does it surprise you that God would allow it?

It might be time for a change in perspective. May I suggest a mission trip to a country where persecution of believers is a way of life? If you simply cannot go on one of those trips, use today as an opportunity to sign up for information from Voice of the Martyrs or another organization that ministers to those who experience real persecution.

Commit to praying for our brothers and sisters who are in those areas of difficulty. Remember to pray for our country, which is heading down a path of increasing hostility. In light of this, pray that the Lord will give you courage in these, the last days, to take a true stand for His kingdom. Each time you do, may the Lord continue to strengthen you.

"These things I have spoken to you, so that in
Me you may have peace.
In the world you have tribulation,
but take courage; I have overcome the world."
—JOHN 16:33

My Task/Challenge

_____

_____

_____

_____

_____

_____

_____

_____

_____

_____

My Outcome/Results

_____

_____

_____

_____

_____

_____

_____

_____

_____

_____

DAY 41 ~ *One Body—One Lord*

Remember that you were at that time separate from Christ, excluded from the commonwealth of Israel, and strangers to the covenants of promise, having no hope and without God in the world.
—EPHESIANS 2:12

When I read the above passage, I cannot help but picture Cain, the central figure in an early tragedy in Genesis. Talk about a person who found himself excluded from family blessings, one who became a stranger wherever he went, one who was indeed separated from God—a separation which automatically means a hopeless and hapless life in this world.

Cain committed an unspeakable act that resulted from internal jealousy and anger. Cain murdered his younger brother, Abel. Warned by God to master his emotions before they could master him, Cain ignored the warning and not only killed his brother and attempted to hide the deed from the Lord but also lied to God when given a chance to repent.[182] His response to the Lord when asked where his brother was might well have been, *"Abel? Abel? What's an Abel?"* What came next was certain and swift judgment.

Then the LORD said to Cain, "Where is Abel your brother?" And he said, "I do not know. Am I my brother's keeper?"

He said, "What have you done? The voice of your brother's blood is crying to Me from the ground. Now you are cursed from the ground, which has opened its mouth to receive your brother's blood from your hand. When you cultivate the ground, it will no longer yield its strength to you; you will be a vagrant and a wanderer on the earth."

Cain said to the LORD, "My punishment is too great to bear! Behold, You have driven me this day from the

---

[182] Genesis 4:9

face of the ground; and from Your face I will be hidden, and I will be a vagrant and a wanderer on the earth, and whoever finds me will kill me."

So the LORD said to him, "Therefore whoever kills Cain, vengeance will be taken on him sevenfold." And the LORD appointed a sign for Cain, so that no one finding him would slay him. Then Cain went out from the presence of the LORD, and settled in the land of Nod, east of Eden.[183]

When I think of Cain's punishment—his separation from the ability to truly worship and shunning by his family—I cannot help but think of the Samaritan people. They seemed to be people with no hope in the world. The Jews shunned them, viewing them as half-breeds since they were the descendants of Jews who mixed with pagan nations. Yet an alert came to them. The Messiah had arrived and was in their own country. With that news and their enthusiastic response, the Samaritan people went from hopelessness to a relationship with God Himself.

Many of the Samaritans believed in Him based upon the testimony of the woman at the well. She affirmed, "He told me all the things that I have done."[184] Therefore, when the Samaritans came to Jesus, they implored Him to stay with them, which He did for two days. The great news is:

Many more believed because of His word; and they were saying to the woman, "It is no longer because of what you said that we believe, for we have heard for ourselves and know that this One is indeed the Savior of the world."[185]

What happened to the Samaritan people is a beautiful picture of individuals who realized the transformation of our opening verse, whose lives changed for time and eternity. It is the adoption of a people who were once as far from God as they could be, welcomed into His heavenly family. What Cain would never

---

[183] Genesis 4:9–16
[184] John 2:29
[185] John 4:39–42

know, the Samaritan people did, and so do all those who are Gentiles by birth but adopted into the family of God.[186]

In the Book of Ephesians, Paul accurately described the hopelessness in the lost state of Gentiles. Yet, they were brought into the family of God thanks to the Jewish Messiah, through whom both groups have salvation:

> But now in Christ Jesus you who formerly were far off have been brought near by the blood of Christ. For He Himself is our peace, who made both groups into one and broke down the barrier of the dividing wall, by abolishing in His flesh the enmity, which is the Law of commandments contained in ordinances, so that in Himself He might make the two into one new man, thus establishing peace, and might reconcile them both in one body to God through the cross, by it having put to death the enmity.[187]

What a beautiful picture! Paul stated in 1 Corinthians:

> For even as the body is one and yet has many members, and all the members of the body, though they are many, are one body, so also is Christ. For by one Spirit we were all baptized into one body, whether Jews or Greeks, whether slaves or free, and we were all made to drink of one Spirit.[188]

We were once far off, but now we are family. There is no distinction between Jew and Gentile or any other ethnic or cultural or societal grouping; we are one in Jesus, our Lord, Yeshua the Messiah of Israel. Do you see that? Do you feel that when you are with believers or do you look for what divides you, like nonessential particulars of worship or other aspects of our expressions of faith in Him?

Are you one who feels arrogant toward Jewish people for missing their Messiah? God ordained that so the Gentiles would have hope! Their time for salvation will come.[189] Do you identify

---

[186] Ephesians 2:12
[187] Ephesians 2:13–16
[188] 1 Corinthians 12:12–13
[189] Zechariah 12:8–10

yourself as a Messianic Jew and look down your nose at the Gentile believer, imagining you have one up on him or her? Get that thinking out of your head right now. Your Jewishness did not save you; the Messiah did.

Weigh your heart and attitude today. Since you were at one time far off and are now near, perhaps the best attitude to embrace would be one of humility and gratitude. After all, imagine where you would be had you not been "brought near" by the blood of Christ.

For there is no distinction between Jew and Greek;
for the same Lord is Lord of all,
abounding in riches for all who call on Him; for
"WHOEVER WILL CALL ON THE NAME OF THE LORD
WILL BE SAVED."
—ROMANS 10:12–13

My Task/Challenge

_____
_____
_____
_____
_____
_____
_____
_____
_____
_____
_____

My Outcome/Results

_____
_____
_____
_____
_____
_____
_____
_____
_____
_____
_____
_____

DAY 42 ~ *Imprisoned Yet Free*

Remember Jesus Christ, risen from the dead,
descendant of David, according to my gospel,
for which I suffer hardship even to imprisonment as a criminal;
but the word of God is not imprisoned.
—2 TIMOTHY 2:8–9

What a fantastic reminder today's opening verse is! The apostle Paul, in his admonition to young Timothy, reminds us that no matter where we are, no matter how great the desire of those hostile to the gospel might be to silence or even imprison us, God's Word is not subject to any kind of imprisonment or captivity.

Throughout the Scriptures, we find this truth. In Genesis 39, we read:

> The chief jailer committed to Joseph's charge all the prisoners who were in the jail; so that whatever was done there, he was responsible for it. The chief jailer did not supervise anything under Joseph's charge because the LORD was with him; and whatever he did, the LORD made to prosper.[190]

Not only was Joseph granted divine favor with the jailor, but while in prison, he experienced the God-given ability to interpret dreams, whereby he was able to communicate the fate of a particular royal baker and chief cup-bearer. The accuracy of the interpretations given to him by God put him face-to-face with Pharaoh, where, once again, Joseph found great favor and blessing.

We also read about Daniel. Though he was in Babylonian captivity, he continued to stand by God's Word,

---

[190] Genesis 39:22–23

uncompromisingly communicating the interpretation of another kingly dream, one which ultimately led to that king's salvation.[191]

Then there was Jeremiah, the prophet, who found himself imprisoned under Zedekiah, Judah's king.[192] God's Word was not imprisoned in his case, either. When Zedekiah questioned Jeremiah as to the Lord's Word for Judah, he felt compelled to speak what God impressed upon him, which was not the best of news.

We can also recall John the Baptist, who did not remain silent when imprisoned by Herod. In Mark's account, we read that:

> Herod was afraid of John, knowing that he was a righteous and holy man, and he kept him safe. And when he heard him, he was very perplexed; but he used to enjoy listening to him.[193]

John the Baptist spoke uncompromisingly and consistently the message of repentance for the forgiveness of sins and turning to the Messiah as the only answer.

Throughout the book of Acts, we see that God's Word did not suffer imprisonment during the New Covenant era either. God mightily used His Word in the lives of those who proclaimed and heard it.

It is especially interesting that the very one who imprisoned so many for proclaiming Yeshua as Lord would himself eventually be imprisoned for the same reason. The apostle Paul, who penned the opening words for today, had quite the prison ministry. It is incredible the number of influential people Paul was able to speak to under the inspiration of the Holy Spirit during his times of arrest.

From Felix to Festus, Ananias to Agrippa, from a Philippian jailor to a centurion commander, Paul made an impact and impression. The apostle Paul obediently left each person he met with no doubt as to the fact that God's Word lives on and that the weightiest news humanity could ever receive was the news of Yeshua, raised from the dead, having paid the penalty for the sin of the world.

---

[191] Daniel 4
[192] Jeremiah 32:2–3
[193] Mark 6:20

What a testimony this is for us. Through all hardship, even prison, we are to remember Yeshua, who rose from the dead, and we are to proclaim that message to others. Because God's Word is as alive inside the prison as it is outside, it does not matter where we are. God will grant us just the right words and a unique opportunity to share it.

Has this been your experience? Have you ever been in an environment where you asked yourself, *"How could God be glorified in this place, or this situation, or with these people?"* Our great God makes an impact in places where many believers would never imagine finding Him. We need to face this fact. We need to stop cowering behind the couch when the doorbell rings with a cultist eager to speak lies.

We need to stop shying away from opportunities to speak out in public places. We need to believe that even when we are face-to-face with folks who can silence us for good, we should be praying for their soul and for the courage and opportunity to speak as He would have us. Trust Him; if you are willing, He is ready to give you His Word, no matter where you are or before whom you are to speak. Are you willing? Commit to proclaiming His Word today.

I will also speak of Your testimonies
before kings and shall not be ashamed.
—PSALM 119:46

My Task/Challenge

_____

_____

_____

_____

_____

_____

_____

_____

_____

My Outcome/Results

_____

_____

_____

_____

_____

_____

_____

_____

_____

_____

DAY 43 ~ *A Fool for Christ*

But remember the former days, when, after being enlightened,
you endured a great conflict of sufferings,
partly by being made a public spectacle through reproaches and
tribulations, and partly by becoming sharers
with those who were so treated.
—HEBREWS 10:32–33

wo individuals immediately come to mind when I think of today's passage. The first is Noah. The Lord God enlightened Noah to the fact that He was going to judge all wickedness upon the earth with a worldwide flood while sparing Noah and his small family. Therefore, it was time to spend the next 120 years in the barge building business.

Can you imagine a man in that day building a vessel 450-feet long, 75-feet wide, and 45-feet high, with only his three sons to help him and nowhere to launch it? I don't think we can fathom the effort it took to embark on such a task, no matter how hard Hollywood tries. Moreover, what did the neighbors think of this spectacle? Can you imagine the thoughts going through the minds and out the mouths of those nefarious people? We know that no amount of reproaches and tribulations deterred Noah and his sons since Genesis 6 ends with the words, "Thus Noah did; according to all that God had commanded him, so he did."[194]

Just imagine the mocking Noah and his sons endured. Perhaps folks might even have tried to sabotage the project. In the face of it all, an undeterred, faithful Noah kept up the building project. With every insult they hurled at him, I'm sure his comeback was a stern warning for them to get building as well. Since Noah was a righteous man, he would have also been concerned for their souls.

Unfortunately, the fun and games at Noah's expense ended when that gentile *drip, drip, drip* from the sky turned into torrents of rain, with the very chasms of the deep bursting forth to flood

---

[194] Genesis 6:22

the entire earth as detailed on Day 16. Before they knew it, the townsfolk would drown and their mocking words with them while Noah and his family stayed safe and dry.

The second individual who comes to mind is Joshua, a man who conquered a city most unconventionally. Nevertheless, when the Lord tells you to do something, you had best obey even if it appears a bit quirky:

> The LORD said to Joshua, "See, I have given Jericho into your hand, with its king and the valiant warriors. You shall march around the city, all the men of war circling the city once. You shall do so for six days.
>
> "Also seven priests shall carry seven trumpets of rams' horns before the ark; then on the seventh day you shall march around the city seven times, and the priests shall blow the trumpets. It shall be that when they make a long blast with the ram's horn, and when you hear the sound of the trumpet, all the people shall shout with a great shout; and the wall of the city will fall down flat, and the people will go up every man straight ahead."[195]

I think the most attention-getting part of God's command is the very first word: He told Joshua to *see* the city already conquered as God saw it. What a fantastic thing it is to have God's perspective and favor in the face of the impossible! However, Joshua had to have the faith that what God commanded for victory would work. General Joshua must have realized how out of the norm this command was as a military tactic. Whoever heard of conquering a city by marching around its impenetrable walls for a week, then blowing horns and shouting at it? I'm sure, after receiving their orders, some of his men must have stared at each other, thinking, *Did we just hear the command we thought we heard?*

The people of Jericho must have gotten a good chuckle too, thinking it silly for those Hebrew soldiers to march around their impenetrable walls with a handful of priests for seven days. However, just as in Noah's case, right around the time the people shouted, the laughing stopped. The public spectacle was funny no

---

[195] Joshua 6:2–5

longer as Joshua and his army, in obedience to God's unexpected military tactic, conquered Jericho.

What a lost world ridicules is what the Lord desires to use for His glory. The author of Hebrews suggested that when this happens in our lives, we become "sharers with those who were so treated" in the past.

After Noah and Joshua, the supreme event for ridicule would come, and yet it was the apex of God's wisdom:

> For the word of the cross is foolishness to those who are perishing, but to us who are being saved it is the power of God. For it is written, "I will destroy the wisdom of the wise, and the cleverness of the clever I will set aside."
>
> Where is the wise man? Where is the scribe? Where is the debater of this age? Has not God made foolish the wisdom of the world? For since in the wisdom of God the world through its wisdom did not come to know God, God was well pleased through the foolishness of the message preached to save those who believe.
>
> For indeed Jews ask for signs and Greeks search for wisdom; but we preach Christ crucified, to Jews a stumbling block and to Gentiles foolishness, but to those who are the called, both Jews and Greeks, Christ the power of God and the wisdom of God. Because the foolishness of God is wiser than men, and the weakness of God is stronger than men.[196]

As in Noah's day, God's ark for salvation is an object of ridicule for lost individuals. We, like Noah, Joshua, and all those who put themselves under the authority of God to obey Him, do and say things the world believes is foolish. The Lord, through our preaching, attempts to rescue them from the fate they'll face for standing by the ridicule they spew.

Today's question, and the challenge is this; are you willing to be foolish for the cross? Will you risk being a public spectacle if that is what the Lord requires of you for a great victory in Him? Perhaps

---

[196] 1 Corinthians 1:18–25

you are too worried about what people think. Do you truly believe the reality of their fate if you do not respond as He calls you? Are you wavering? If so, remember those who obeyed. Remember what their obedience led to, and do not be afraid of becoming sharers with those who were so treated, especially since the One ridiculed more than any other was our Lord Jesus Christ.

For the wisdom of this world is foolishness before God.
For it is written, "He is THE ONE WHO CATCHES
THE WISE IN THEIR CRAFTINESS"; and again, "THE LORD KNOWS
THE REASONINGS OF THE WISE, THAT THEY ARE USELESS."
—1 CORINTHIANS 3:19–20

My Task/Challenge

_____
_____
_____
_____
_____
_____
_____
_____
_____
_____
_____

My Outcome/Results

_____
_____
_____
_____
_____
_____
_____
_____
_____
_____
_____
_____

DAY 44 ~ *Radical Redemptions*

For consider Him who has endured such hostility
by sinners against Himself,
so that you will not grow weary and lose heart.
—HEBREWS 12:3

The constant threat of facing hostility can undoubtedly make one lose heart. When we consider the hatred of the Chaldeans who could not wait to accuse Daniel's compatriots, Hananiah, Mishael, and Azariah, of ignoring the golden statue worship of King Nebuchadnezzar, it was clear that things would soon get dicey. If ever there were young men who faced an occasion to grow weary of doing well, that was it.

After having gone into captivity, Hananiah, Mishael, and Azariah found themselves with new Chaldean names and targets on their backs. Because of Daniel's ability to tell King Nebuchadnezzar the details of a particular dream he'd had and what it meant, he suddenly found himself elevated to a prominent position. Daniel's prominent post was one thing, but that his friends also held elevated positions was something that did not square too well with the local worldly-wise men.

> The king promoted Daniel and gave him many great gifts, and he made him ruler over the whole province of Babylon and chief prefect over all the wise men of Babylon. And Daniel made request of the king, and he appointed Shadrach, Meshach and Abed-nego over the administration of the province of Babylon, while Daniel was at the king's court.[197]

It would not be long before Daniel's friends would learn whether their faith in God would genuinely stand the test. After a few modifications to the original design he remembered from his

---

[197] Daniel 2:48–49

dream, Nebuchadnezzar had a statue erected for all to worship, including the newly promoted captives. However, they refused to kneel before the figure. Because of their refusal, the king, with rage in his eyes, told Shadrach, Meshach, and Abed-nego to bow or bake. Upon this choice, the three casually replied:

> "O Nebuchadnezzar, we do not need to give you an answer concerning this matter. If it be so, our God whom we serve is able to deliver us from the furnace of blazing fire; and He will deliver us out of your hand, O king. But even if He does not, let it be known to you, O king, that we are not going to serve your gods or worship the golden image that you have set up."[198]

Talk about taking a bold stand before King Nebuchadnezzar! Because of this, into the furnace, they went. But they were not alone. To the utter dismay of all onlookers, a fourth Man became visible in the furnace with them. Upon seeing such a sight, the king frantically called them to come out. The Babylonians then realized that "the fire had no effect on the bodies of these men nor was the hair of their head singed, nor were their trousers damaged, nor had the smell of fire even come upon them."[199]

Who was this Individual in the fiery furnace with Daniel's friends—this mysterious *Fourth Man*? What they experienced, many scholars believe, was a *Christophany*—an appearance of the pre-incarnate Christ, Yeshua, the Messiah. I imagine that after walking with Yeshua in that furnace, they were strengthened to the point that no matter what happened to them in captivity, they would "not grow weary and lose heart."[200] Those captive men learned quickly that the Lord was with them in their circumstances.

Apparently, He takes to heart the hostility individuals have toward those who love Him. We see this again in the case of Saul of Tarsus. Of this man, who was in "hearty agreement"[201] with Stephen's stoning (the first martyr of the Faith), we read that immediately following that tragic event, "Saul began ravaging the church, entering house after house, and dragging off men and

---

[198] Daniel 3:16–18
[199] Daniel 3:27
[200] Hebrews 12:3
[201] Acts 8:1

women, he would put them in prison."[202] His hostility in full gear, he gained permission to search for followers of the Way north into Syria—that is, until his dramatic conversion:

> Now Saul, still breathing threats and murder against the disciples of the Lord, went to the high priest, and asked for letters from him to the synagogues at Damascus, so that if he found any belonging to the Way, both men and women, he might bring them bound to Jerusalem. As he was traveling, it happened that he was approaching Damascus, and suddenly a light from heaven flashed around him; and he fell to the ground and heard a voice saying to him, "Saul, Saul, why are you persecuting Me?"
>
> And he said, "Who are You, Lord?"
>
> And He said, "I am Jesus whom you are persecuting, but get up and enter the city, and it will be told you what you must do."[203]

Did you notice that? Jesus did not say, "I am Jesus, the One folks follow whom you are persecuting," but rather, "I am Jesus whom you are persecuting." When people express hostility toward us, it is the same as expressing hostility toward Him. That is our personal Lord and Savior! Yet, we see God's grace poured out upon Saul, who became the apostle Paul and wrote most of the New Testament. We also find His incredible grace poured out on an arrogant king who went from throwing believers into a furnace in Daniel 3 to proclaiming his faith in the Most High God by Daniel 4. The Lord is a loving, forgiving God.

When we consider the salvation the Lord God brought to Nebuchadnezzar and Saul, we realize there is hope for those who persecute with hostility, even to the point of committing murder. Is anyone beyond His grasp? Of course not.

Today, realize that if we keep our eyes on Him, we will not grow weary and lose heart—and our godly perseverance before the hostile just might allow us to celebrate with them in glory. Stay heartened, be diligent in prayer, and keep your eyes on Jesus, Who

---

[202] Acts 8:3
[203] Acts 9:1–6

can transform those individuals who hate you, and thus Him, from a Saul to a Paul.

Now when the centurion saw what had happened,
he began praising God, saying, "Certainly this man was innocent."
—LUKE 23:47

My Task/Challenge

_____
_____
_____
_____
_____
_____
_____
_____
_____
_____

My Outcome/Results

_____
_____
_____
_____
_____
_____
_____
_____
_____
_____
_____

DAY 45 ~ *Remember the Prisoners*

Remember the prisoners, as though in prison with them,
and those who are ill-treated,
since you yourselves also are in the body.
—HEBREWS 13:3

*W*hen I think of those who were mistreated and imprisoned, once again, I have to consider Jeremiah the prophet. Always being faithful to speak the Lord's words, he proclaimed a warning to the people of Jerusalem to get out of the city while they could. Yet all his warnings that the Chaldeans were coming seemed to be of no avail. Instead of listening to Jeremiah's warning, the city officials accused him of evil intentions for discouraging the people with bad news. They requested that king Zedekiah allow them to make quick disposal of the Weeping Prophet.

With permission granted, the officials felt the best way to dispose of him quietly would be to imprison him in an empty cistern. So there went the prophet of God, lowered by a rope into a wet, dark hole in the ground. As he sank further, his body became stuck in the cold mud. Can you imagine how horrible this imprisonment would be?

The purpose of Jeremiah's enemies was to ensure that he would die a miserable, cold, hungry, obscure death without the chance to proclaim any last words of an additional warning to the people. However, there was one brave man who would not forget the prisoner—a man who was well aware of the unjust treatment of God's prophet—a man who was not even of the commonwealth of Israel.

But Ebed-melech the Ethiopian, a eunuch, while he was in the king's palace, heard that they had put Jeremiah into the cistern. Now the king was sitting in the Gate of Benjamin; and Ebed-melech went out from the king's palace and spoke to the king, saying, "My lord the king, these men have acted wickedly in all that they have done to Jeremiah the prophet whom they have cast into the cistern; and he will die right where he is because of the famine, for there is no more bread in the city."

Then the king commanded Ebed-melech the Ethiopian, saying, "Take thirty men from here under your authority and bring up Jeremiah the prophet from the cistern before he dies."[204]

Ebed-melech must have been an incredibly compassionate and brave man. To go to the king and tell him squarely that this treatment of Jeremiah was wicked was an amazingly courageous act. This Ethiopian could easily have found himself neck-deep in the mire along with Jeremiah. Despite the risk, he remembered the prisoner and saw to it that he saved his life. For his brave act, once Jerusalem's conquering ensued, as prophesied by Jeremiah, we read the following:

The word of the LORD had come to Jeremiah while he was confined in the court of the guardhouse, saying, "Go and speak to Ebed-melech the Ethiopian, saying, 'Thus says the LORD of hosts, the God of Israel, "Behold, I am about to bring My words on this city for disaster and not for prosperity; and they will take place before you on that day. But I will deliver you on that day," declares the LORD, "and you will not be given into the hand of the men whom you dread. For I will certainly rescue you, and you will not fall by the sword; but you will have your own life as booty, because you have trusted in Me," declares the LORD.'"[205]

That faithful man, Ebed-melech, received deliverance, which is more than we can say for King Zedekiah. Later, there would be another unforgotten prisoner—one who received great encouragement that his preaching was not in vain.

There sat John the Baptist in Herod's prison. Yet he was not alone. Some individuals not only remembered him but went so far as to inquire of Jesus on his behalf:

---

[204] Jeremiah 38:7–10
[205] Jeremiah 39:15–18

Now when John, while imprisoned, heard of the works of Christ, he sent word by his disciples and said to Him, "Are You the Expected One, or shall we look for someone else?"

Jesus answered and said to them, "Go and report to John what you hear and see: the blind receive sight and the lame walk, the lepers are cleansed and the deaf hear, the dead are raised up, and the poor have the gospel preached to them. And blessed is he who does not take offense at Me."[206]

What an example John's disciples were! In John's brief moment of questioning, they were not fearful or ashamed to visit him while he was Herod's prisoner. The visitors who conveyed Jesus's message to John must have strengthened his resolve tremendously by Jesus's confirming words.

The Lord sent a message of encouragement to John through John's disciples. Will you allow Him to use you to make an impact in some way for a prisoner today? I once received a letter from a woman across the country, who was confined to prison. While there, someone remembered her imprisonment and offered her my book, *Reasons for Faith*. She wrote in her letter that she was so encouraged by it that she wanted other women to read it as well. That so blessed my heart, I wound up sending a whole case to the prison! Though I couldn't be there in person because of the distance, it was simply my way of visiting them.

Seek Him in this area and allow Him to use you as He sees fit to touch the lives of the imprisoned, whether justly or unjustly. You never realize what an impact you can make.

For He looked down from His holy height;
from heaven the LORD gazed upon the earth,
to hear the groaning of the prisoner,
to set free those who were doomed to death,
that men may tell of the name of the LORD in
Zion and His praise in Jerusalem.
— PSALM 102:19–21

---

[206] Matthew 11:2–6

My Task/Challenge

My Outcome/Results

DAY 46 ~ *Passing the Torch*

Remember those who led you, who spoke the word of God to you;
and considering the result of their conduct, imitate their faith.
—HEBREWS 13:7

*H*ow blessed it is to have a godly example to follow, and how blessed it is to be able to pass that torch! Elijah and Elisha experienced this, though at first, Elijah believed he was alone in his zeal for God. How wrong Elijah was!

On Day 21, we read how the prophet Elijah became exhausted, going from the pinnacle of his success to being physically drained and emotionally fearful. In a cave at Horeb, Elijah heard God speak, away from the threats of his enemies and the turmoil of the city. He heard words that would encourage him that help was on the way. One of the things God informed Elijah in that special and unique moment was, "Elisha the son of Shaphat of Abel-meholah you shall anoint as prophet in your place."[207] It was time for Elijah to pass the torch, or rather, the mantle:

> So he departed from there and found Elisha the son of Shaphat, while he was plowing with twelve pairs of oxen before him, and he with the twelfth. And Elijah passed over to him and threw his mantle on him. He left the oxen and ran after Elijah and said, "Please let me kiss my father and my mother, then I will follow you."
>
> And he said to him, "Go back again, for what have I done to you?" So he returned from following him, and took the pair of oxen and sacrificed them and boiled their flesh with the implements of the oxen, and gave it to the people and they ate. Then he arose and followed Elijah and ministered to him.[208]

---

[207] 1 Kings 19:16
[208] 1 Kings 19:19–21

Though Elisha went back to have one last sacrificial feast with his family, he was eager to say good-bye. He did not hesitate to follow in the footsteps of Elijah, a man who happened to have an angry, depraved queen out for his head. By 2 Kings 2, we see that this one who had learned well from his mentor refused to leave Elijah's side. Yet the time would eventually come when Elisha would carry on the ministry by himself:

Elijah said to Elisha, "Ask what I shall do for you before I am taken from you."

And Elisha said, "Please, let a double portion of your spirit be upon me."

He said, "You have asked a hard thing. Nevertheless, if you see me when I am taken from you, it shall be so for you; but if not, it shall not be so."

As they were going along and talking, behold, there appeared a chariot of fire and horses of fire which separated the two of them. And Elijah went up by a whirlwind to heaven. Elisha saw it and cried out, "My father, my father, the chariots of Israel and its horsemen!" And he saw Elijah no more. Then he took hold of his own clothes and tore them in two pieces.[209]

The pathos expressed by Elisha upon seeing Elijah disappear from his sight should cut deep into our hearts. Elisha knew the day had come, yet no one is fully prepared to say goodbye to his or her beloved mentor. Such must have been the case for young Timothy when receiving the last letter Paul would ever pen. How wonderful it is that we have those words recorded in Second Timothy! It makes me wonder what final words Elijah and Elisha exchanged as they crossed the Jordan on dry ground. Perhaps in glory, we will find out.

As we think of the mentor relationship, we cannot help but consider our Lord and His conversation with Peter as they broke bread and enjoyed freshly broiled fish for a shoreline breakfast one morning after Yeshua's resurrection.[210]

---

[209] 2 Kings 2:9–12
[210] John 21:15–17

Jesus requested that Peter verbally confirm his love for Him. Three times He asked this of Peter, and after each response came, "Tend My lambs," then "Shepherd My sheep," and finally, "Tend My sheep." Perhaps Jesus had Peter confirm his love for Him three times as a way to cancel out Peter's three denials of even knowing Him. Jesus's commands, after Peter's confirmations of love, would reinforce for Peter his new task of tending the Lord's people.

The mentor moments outlined in the Scriptures expose unique bonds. These are vital relationships. No matter how old we are, no matter how advanced we are in our walk with the Lord, there are still people around us who have walked with Him longer and are more mature. Do you have the privilege of this kind of relationship in your life? We are not to imitate the flaws of our mentors—we already have our own—but we are to imitate their faith. Cherish those relationships. You never know how long they will last before the Lord calls them home.

Are you, or have you been, discipled? Do you disciple the people you lead to the Lord? Do you make yourself available and open to disciple others? If not, why not?

Perhaps you see how important it is that you have a mentor. Today, consider whom the Lord would have you emulate. Whose feet can you figuratively sit at to glean from their wisdom? Then as you learn, remember that you too may fill that all-important role in someone else's life. Is there anyone around you who needs an Elijah or a Paul?

So the LORD said to Moses, "Take Joshua the son of Nun, a man in whom is the Spirit, and lay your hand on him; and have him stand before Eleazar the priest and before all the congregation, and commission him in their sight. You shall put some of your authority on him, in order that all the congregation of the sons of Israel may obey him."
—NUMBERS 27:18–20

My Task/Challenge

_____
_____
_____
_____
_____
_____
_____
_____
_____
_____
_____
_____

My Outcome/Results

_____
_____
_____
_____
_____
_____
_____
_____
_____
_____
_____
_____

DAY 47 ~ *The Importance of Repentance*

I am stirring up your sincere mind by way of reminder, that you should remember the words spoken beforehand by the holy prophets and the commandment of the Lord and Savior spoken by your apostles.
—2 PETER 3:1–2

As we near the end of our fifty-day devotional, I think it is evident that the core message of the Old Covenant is the same as that of the New. There is consistency in God's Word, and as we will learn today, the primary message of the prophets of our Lord and the apostles was one of repentance for the forgiveness of sins.

We see the impact and importance of repentance in the following excerpt from Solomon's dedication prayer in the newly built Temple as he stood before the altar of the Lord:

"When they [the people of Israel] sin against You (for there is no man who does not sin) and You are angry with them and deliver them to an enemy, so that they take them away captive to the land of the enemy, far off or near; if they take thought in the land where they have been taken captive, and repent and make supplication to You in the land of those who have taken them captive, saying, 'We have sinned and have committed iniquity, we have acted wickedly'; if they return to You with all their heart and with all their soul in the land of their enemies who have taken them captive, and pray to You toward their land which You have given to their fathers, the city which You have chosen, and the house which I have built for Your name; then hear their prayer and their supplication in heaven Your dwelling place, and maintain their cause, and forgive Your people who have sinned against You and all their transgressions which they have transgressed against You, and make them objects of

210

compassion before those who have taken them captive, that they may have compassion on them."[211]

In Ezekiel 18, we find Ezekiel the prophet proclaiming the following words of the Lord:

> "When a wicked man turns away from his wickedness which he has committed and practices justice and righteousness, he will save his life. Because he considered and turned away from all his transgressions which he had committed, he shall surely live; he shall not die."[212]

This call to repentance is consistent throughout the Scriptures. Matthew 3:1–2 reads, "Now in those days John the Baptist came, preaching in the wilderness of Judea, saying, 'Repent, for the kingdom of heaven is at hand.'"

Jesus's declaration was utterly consistent with John's: "From that time Jesus began to preach and say, 'Repent, for the kingdom of heaven is at hand.'"[213]

In Luke's account, Jesus explained His purpose to the professional religious people of the day:

> The Pharisees and their scribes began grumbling at His disciples, saying, "Why do you eat and drink with the tax collectors and sinners?"

> And Jesus answered and said to them, "It is not those who are well who need a physician, but those who are sick. I have not come to call the righteous but sinners to repentance."[214]

To call sinners to repentance—that was Yeshua's purpose. That is why He came as one of us, preached among us, died for us, and resurrected to glory. We are all sinners who need to repent. Many individuals proclaim Yeshua but miss the significance of true repentance. There needs to be a genuine about-face from our sins.

---

[211] 1 Kings 8:46–50
[212] Ezekiel 18:27-28
[213] Matthew 4:17
[214] Luke 5:30–32

I struggled with this for years before giving Jesus my life at twenty-eight years old. I never realized how important it was to turn away from my sins. I did not fully understand that what kept me from a place of blessed peace in my soul was my tenacious clinging to *my* way. Once I confessed and turned from the sins that kept me at arm's length from the Lord, I knew He forgave me and that my home was with Him.

Is repentance a message you stress when sharing the gospel? People need to know! I had a flawed view of my responsibility as a professing believer for ten years because no one ever explained the need to repent and make a complete turnaround from my sins. What I always seemed to hear was, "As long as you prayed the prayer, you're there!" What a dangerous thing to miss and yet still refer to yourself as "born again," as I did for ten floundering years.

If you have yet to embrace the significance of repentance for the forgiveness of your sins, embrace it today. Own it. Do not miss this as you present the gospel to others. If it was important enough for Solomon, Ezekiel, John the Baptist, and Jesus, it is just as important for you. The consequences of not communicating the necessity of repentance are far too great.

The Lord is not slow about His promise, as some count slowness, but is patient toward you, not wishing for any to perish but for all to come to repentance.
—2 PETER 3:9

My Task/Challenge

_____

_____

_____

_____

_____

_____

_____

_____

_____

_____

My Outcome/Results

_____

_____

_____

_____

_____

_____

_____

_____

_____

_____

_____

DAY 48 ~ *God is Not Mocked*

---

*But you, beloved, ought to remember the words that were
spoken beforehand by the apostles of our Lord Jesus Christ,
that they were saying to you, "In the last time there will be mockers,
following after their own ungodly lusts."*
—JUDE 17–18

There have always been mockers. As outlined over these
many days of devotion, there were plenty of ridiculers
throughout the Old Covenant. One such individual was
King Belshazzar of Babylon—the heir of King Nebuchadnezzar. This
fellow thought it would be a good idea to take items consecrated
for the worship of God in the Temple of God and use them as
party favors:

> Belshazzar, the king, held a great feast for a thousand
> of his nobles, and he was drinking wine in the presence of
> the thousand. When Belshazzar tasted the wine, he gave
> orders to bring the gold and silver vessels which
> Nebuchadnezzar his father had taken out of the temple
> which was in Jerusalem, so that the king and his nobles,
> his wives and his concubines might drink from them.
>
> Then they brought the gold vessels that had been
> taken out of the temple, the house of God which was in
> Jerusalem; and the king and his nobles, his wives and his
> concubines drank from them. They drank the wine and
> praised the gods of gold and silver, of bronze, iron, wood
> and stone.[215]

A good time was had by all—until:

> Suddenly the fingers of a man's hand emerged and
> began writing opposite the lampstand on the plaster of
> the wall of the king's palace, and the king saw the back of
> the hand that did the writing. Then the king's face grew

---

[215] Daniel 5:1–4

pale and his thoughts alarmed him, and his hip joints went slack and his knees began knocking together.[216]

That hand, as it wrote, was quite a party crasher, and I imagine it sobered them up pretty quickly! The finger of God had appeared and sealed the man's fate. Belshazzar's mother, King Nebuchadnezzar's widow, summoned Daniel once again to interpret what they could not. In the process of interpreting the writing on the wall, Daniel did something significant. He reminded Belshazzar of his father's testimony of conversion. He also reminded him of the fact that Belshazzar himself refused to emulate his father, the king's faith. He then explained the ominous inscription:

"This is the interpretation of the message: 'MENE'—God has numbered your kingdom and put an end to it. 'TEKEL'—you have been weighed on the scales and found deficient. 'PERES'—your kingdom has been divided and given over to the Medes and Persians."

Then Belshazzar gave orders, and they clothed Daniel with purple and put a necklace of gold around his neck, and issued a proclamation concerning him that he now had authority as the third ruler in the kingdom. That same night Belshazzar the Chaldean king was slain.[217]

Perhaps Belshazzar thought that by giving Daniel gifts and promotion, he would find favor and that frightening prophecy would not come true. *Maybe if I'm nice to the old Jewish guy, this won't happen to me.* People who shake their fists at God never think anything is going to happen to them. They are bold and brazen, but in the end, their lives will be required of them.

If there were "mockers, following after their own ungodly lusts" in Daniel's day, our opening verse informs us that it will get a whole lot worse in these the last days. Jesus warned,

"And just as it happened in the days of Noah, so it will be also in the days of the Son of Man: they were eating, they were drinking, they were marrying, they were being given in marriage, until the day that Noah

[216] Daniel 5:5–6
[217] Daniel 5:26–30

entered the ark, and the flood came and destroyed them all."[218]

Of course, the other important aspect that went with the "days of Noah" was the open immorality of the culture and a complete insensitivity to anything holy or pure. When he wrote of the last days and how people will behave, the Apostle Paul described perfectly what many people are like today. One only needs to turn on the television, or surf the internet, to recognize these attitudes proudly flaunted for all to see:

> But realize this, that in the last days difficult times will come. For men will be lovers of self, lovers of money, boastful, arrogant, revilers, disobedient to parents, ungrateful, unholy, unloving, irreconcilable, malicious gossips, without self-control, brutal, haters of good, treacherous, reckless, conceited, lovers of pleasure rather than lovers of God, holding to a form of godliness, although they have denied its power; avoid such men as these.[219]

There is great advice from Paul at the end of that terrible list: *"Avoid such men as these."* So too, while in the opening verses for today, Jude exposed the problem, he does not leave us there. By divine inspiration, we learn what we are to do as we live in a world of mockers following their lustful ways:

> But you, beloved, building yourselves up on your most holy faith, praying in the Holy Spirit, keep yourselves in the love of God, waiting anxiously for the mercy of our Lord Jesus Christ to eternal life. And have mercy on some, who are doubting; save others, snatching them out of the fire; and on some have mercy with fear, hating even the garment polluted by the flesh.[220]

When you think of Belshazzar and how he cast off his father's faith and witness and then consider the description of how people will behave in the last days, does your mind recall someone you know? If it does, are you navigating that relationship according to

---

[218] Luke 17:26–27
[219] 2 Timothy 3:1–5
[220] Jude 20–23

Jude's advice in these last days? If not, why not? Are you enabling this individual to continue in his or her sin? Do not do it. Be a Daniel and keep reminding such people of the testimony they have witnessed. Follow Jude's advice for each situation. Above all, take a stand. Time is short, and the outcome for the lack of repentance will be grave.

The wicked will not stand in the judgment, nor sinners in the assembly of the righteous. For the LORD knows the way of the righteous, but the way of the wicked will perish.
—PSALM 1:5–6

My Task/Challenge

_____
_____
_____
_____
_____
_____
_____
_____
_____
_____
_____

My Outcome/Results

_____
_____
_____
_____
_____
_____
_____
_____
_____
_____
_____
_____

DAY 49 ~ *Passionate Love vs. Duty*

"You have left your first love. Therefore remember from where you have fallen, and repent and do the deeds you did at first."
—REVELATION 2:4–5

When I think of a first love fading, I consider how Israel began with passion in the days of Joshua. As Joshua recounted God's steadfastness to them through impossible times, he faced the people and squarely challenged their zeal for God. Pay close attention to the responses of the people:

"Now, therefore, fear the LORD and serve Him in sincerity and truth; and put away the gods which your fathers served beyond the River and in Egypt, and serve the LORD. If it is disagreeable in your sight to serve the LORD, choose for yourselves today whom you will serve: whether the gods which your fathers served which were beyond the River, or the gods of the Amorites in whose land you are living; but as for me and my house, we will serve the LORD."

The people answered and said, "Far be it from us that we should forsake the LORD to serve other gods; for the LORD our God is He who brought us and our fathers up out of the land of Egypt, from the house of bondage, and who did these great signs in our sight and preserved us through all the way in which we went and among all the peoples through whose midst we passed. The LORD drove out from before us all the peoples, even the Amorites who lived in the land. We also will serve the LORD, for He is our God."

Then Joshua said to the people, "You will not be able to serve the LORD, for He is a holy God. He is a jealous God; He will not forgive your transgression or your sins. If you forsake the LORD and serve foreign gods, then He will turn and do you harm and consume you after He has done good to you."

219

The people said to Joshua, "No, but we will serve the LORD."

Joshua said to the people, "You are witnesses against yourselves that you have chosen for yourselves the LORD, to serve Him."

And they said, "We are witnesses."

"Now therefore, put away the foreign gods which are in your midst, and incline your hearts to the LORD, the God of Israel."

The people said to Joshua, "We will serve the LORD our God and we will obey His voice."[221]

Joshua and the people of Israel made a clear choice that day. Can you just feel the "*rah-rah*" in the air? Joshua did not impose God upon the people; he simply made a case for how great and mighty the Lord is through the evidence of His many past deeds. Joshua then presented to them an opportunity to choose. The Israelites agreed through their own free will. They all proclaimed, "We will serve the LORD our God, and we will obey His voice." No more discussion needed. Joshua made his choice publicly, and the people made theirs.

We are heartened to read that after Joshua died at the age of 110, "Israel served the LORD all the days of Joshua and all the days of the elders who survived Joshua, and had known all the deeds of the LORD, which He had done for Israel."[222] Yet even so, when we come to the first chapter of the book of Judges, compromise crept in, and soon, the Lord began to rebuke Israel.

So too, our Lord Jesus said to the congregation at Ephesus:

"I know your deeds and your toil and perseverance, and that you cannot tolerate evil men, and you put to the test those who call themselves apostles, and they are not, and you found them to be

---

[221] Joshua 24:14–24
[222] Joshua 24:31

false; and you have perseverance and have endured for My name's sake, and have not grown weary."[223]

The believers in Ephesus were a busy congregation, they were a toiling congregation, and they were a congregation that "examined everything carefully and held fast to that which was good."[224] However, even with all their efforts, Jesus had to rebuke them for leaving their first love. They had a zeal for the things concerning the Lord and His will, but the flame of love had waxed cold, and they didn't even realize it. They did not know that their passions had reduced from loving Christ to going through the motions.

How loving of our Lord to point out to them the things they did right! Notice that along with the rebuke He also told them how to fix their coldness and ignite that fire once again. The cure for them was to go back and remember from where they had fallen and to repent and do the deeds they did when they were first born again into a new life in Him.

We can be just like the church in Ephesus. We need to take the advice Jesus gave them and apply it to ourselves. As with Israel and Joshua, we stand and say with wholehearted zeal, "We are witnesses, as for me and my house, we will serve the LORD." Nevertheless, after a while, that is all it is—service. We reduce our relationship to what we do for God instead of remembering *why* we do it for Him.

Today, go back to that moment when you first came to the Lord. Remember the enthusiasm you had for Jesus, the zeal for God you experienced at your conversion. Go back to those passionate days of gratitude to a Lord Who, when you were dead in your sins, lifted you and seated you in heavenly places with Himself.[225]

Go back and remember what your life was like without Him, then recall in your mind the feeling of Him entering your heart and wiping your slate clean of sin; that moment when you were truly born again, a child of the king. Now, with that level of zeal, go

---

[223] Revelation 2:2–3
[224] 1 Thessalonians 5:21
[225] Ephesians 2:5–6

about the Father's business. Suddenly, you will feel your service to the Lord is not something you do because you have to, but because it is a privilege and honor to serve the One you greatly love.

The LORD appeared to him from afar, saying,
"I have loved you with an everlasting love;
therefore I have drawn you with lovingkindness."
—JEREMIAH 31:3

My Task/Challenge

_____

_____

_____

_____

_____

_____

_____

_____

_____

_____

My Outcome/Results

_____

_____

_____

_____

_____

_____

_____

_____

_____

_____

_____

_____

DAY 50 ~ *Wake Up!*

*"So remember what you have received and heard;
and keep it, and repent.
Therefore if you do not wake up, I will come like a thief,
and you will not know at what hour I will come to you."*
—REVELATION 3:3

Oh, our vulnerability when we are asleep! The above verse is a warning to wake up. Had two individuals not been spiritually asleep at a pivotal time, perhaps they would not have suffered the consequences for the unfortunate timing of their physical sleep.

Samson was the first of these individuals. He had strength beyond compare, but his gift had a secret: it came from a spiritual duty he had followed from birth. Samson's vulnerability toward a woman named Delilah would prove disastrous as she enticed him to disclose the secret to his physical strength. Her goal was not to strengthen their relationship as she proposed, but for a little cash in hand, she desired to pass that secret on to the Philistines. They were enemies of Israel, whom Samson had thrashed more than once. The enemy is still at work even while we are asleep:

> [Delilah] said to [Samson], "How can you say, 'I love you,' when your heart is not with me? You have deceived me these three times and have not told me where your great strength is." It came about when she pressed him daily with her words and urged him, that his soul was annoyed to death.

> So he told her all that was in his heart and said to her, "A razor has never come on my head, for I have been a Nazirite to God from my mother's womb. If I am shaved, then my strength will leave me and I will become weak and be like any other man."

> When Delilah saw that he had told her all that was in his heart, she sent and called the lords of the Philistines,

saying, "Come up once more, for he has told me all that is in his heart." Then the lords of the Philistines came up to her and brought the money in their hands. She made him sleep on her knees, and called for a man and had him shave off the seven locks of his hair. Then she began to afflict him, and his strength left him.

She said, "The Philistines are upon you, Samson!"

And he awoke from his sleep and said, "I will go out as at other times and shake myself free." But he did not know that the LORD had departed from him. Then the Philistines seized him and gouged out his eyes; and they brought him down to Gaza and bound him with bronze chains, and he was a grinder in the prison.[226]

Samson fell for the lie. He snuggled close to the one who turned out to be his enemy, and his false confidence that nothing would ever happen to him gave him the ability to sleep when he should have been wide awake and on his guard. The tragedy was that while he slept soundly, "he did not know that the LORD had departed from him." Ouch!

Then we find Jonah, the second of these individuals, asleep in the hold of a ship, escaping God's call and quite at peace. Going in the opposite direction from where he was supposed to go, he believed that the Lord would not find him. Nevertheless, the Lord would rouse him when he least expected it.

The LORD hurled a great wind on the sea and there was a great storm on the sea so that the ship was about to break up. Then the sailors became afraid and every man cried to his god, and they threw the cargo which was in the ship into the sea to lighten it for them. But Jonah had gone below into the hold of the ship, lain down and fallen sound asleep.

So the captain approached him and said, "How is it that you are sleeping? Get up, call on your god. Perhaps

---

[226] Judges 16:15–21

your god will be concerned about us so that we will not perish."[227]

Even the pagan ship captain knew how inappropriate it was to be sleeping at such a time! Jonah needed to wake up and do what the Lord called him to do. He was to wake up and obey. As we know, Jonah eventually would fulfill his calling and respond with obedience to God. Unfortunately, not under the most ideal of circumstances.

Sadly many people are asleep who need to wake up! Jesus called the church at Sardis to this. His warning to this sleepy congregation was as follows:

> "I know your deeds, that you have a name that you are alive, but you are dead. Wake up, and strengthen the things that remain, which were about to die; for I have not found your deeds completed in the sight of My God.
>
> "So remember what you have received and heard; and keep it, and repent. Therefore if you do not wake up, I will come like a thief, and you will not know at what hour I will come to you . . . He who has an ear, let him hear what the Spirit says to the churches."[228]

This message was not merely for Sardis. It was for anyone who would listen to or read what the Spirit says to all believers. All who name the name of Yeshua, Jesus our Lord, are to "remember what [we] have received and heard; and keep it, and repent." What a simple message!

We have just spent fifty days remembering, considering, and recounting the works of our great God. We have read accounts from the Old Covenant and the New that expose human frailty, God's faithfulness, and His amazing interventions in human weakness. We have witnessed the consequences of obedience and disobedience in the lives of diverse people. At this point, all I can challenge you with is to reiterate what the Lord implored Sardis: *Remember what you have received and heard and keep it,* and when necessary, *repent.*

---

[227] Jonah 1:4–6
[228] To read the letter to Sardis in its entirety, see Revelation 3:1–6.

Because we do not know the hour Jesus will come, let us also be sure we are ready. Are you awake today? Did this devotional help with your waking process? I pray so. Let us always encourage each other with the words of our Lord and the testimony He gives us—always remembering and never forgetting.

"I was asleep but my heart was awake.
A voice! My beloved was knocking."
—SONG OF SOLOMON 5:2

My Task/Challenge

_____
_____
_____
_____
_____
_____
_____
_____
_____
_____
_____

My Outcome/Results

_____
_____
_____
_____
_____
_____
_____
_____
_____
_____
_____
_____

About the Author

*J*udy Salisbury, President and Founder of Logos Presentations, has been equipping Christians to share the gospel more effectively while helping believers to live a vibrant life in the Faith since the start of her multifaceted organization in 1994.

This former radio talk show host has served on her local fire department since 2005 and volunteers as a firefighter, an EMT-I.V., EMS Evaluator, and as the Crisis Care Counselor.

Judy speaks nationally on a wide variety of topics such as Christian living, apologetics, and emotional trauma for secular and faith-based audiences. She is the author of several works including *The Relevance of Revelation*, *Calamity Care*, *Reasons for Faith*, *Engaging Encounters*, and the companion for this work, *The Emmaus Conversation*.

Judy and her husband, Jeff, are proud parents and grandparents. They enjoy an occasional marshmallow roast at their home on the outskirts of Mount St. Helens volcanic National Park in Washington State.

For more information or to schedule
Judy Salisbury for your event, please visit:
www.LogosPresentations.com.

THE EMMAUS CONVERSATION

AN EYEWITNESS ACCOUNT FROM THE UNNAMED DISCIPLE

JUDY SALISBURY

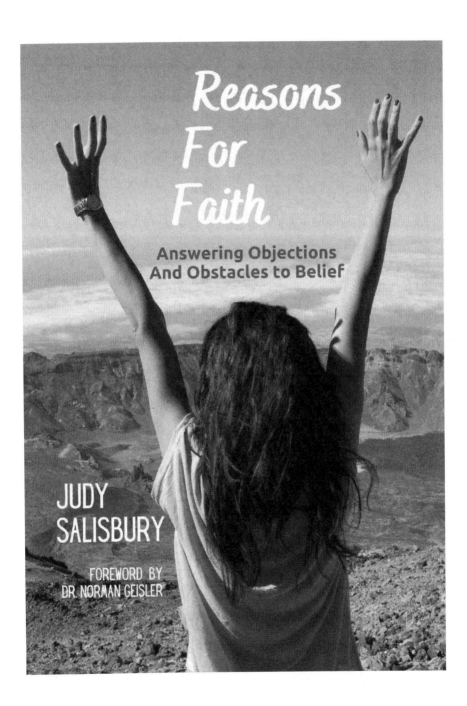

Reasons
For
Faith

Answering Objections
And Obstacles to Belief

JUDY
SALISBURY

FOREWORD BY
DR. NORMAN GEISLER

Engaging Encounters

Your Guide to Apply Reasons for Faith

Judy Salisbury

FOREWORD BY DR. DAVID GEISLER

The Relevance Of Revelation

Thirty-One Days to Radical Revival

JUDY SALISBURY

Calamity Care

My 31-Day Spiritual Guide to Thrive

JUDY SALISBURY

A TIME TO SPEAK

Practical Training For
The Christian Presenter And
The Novice, Nervous, and Neurotic

JUDY SALISBURY

FOREWORD BY
JOSH MCDOWELL

Made in the USA
Columbia, SC
27 April 2022

59530093R00150